KOREAN DANCE, THEATER AND CINEMA

KOREAN DANCE, THEATER AND CINEMA

Edited by
the Korean National Commission for
UNESCO

The Si-sa-yong-o-sa Publishers, Inc., Korea
Pace International Research, Inc., U.S.A.

Published simultaneously in KOREA and the UNITED STATES

KOREA EDITION
First printing 1983
The Si-sa-yong-o-sa Publishers, Inc.
5-3 Kwanchol-dong, Chongno-ku
Seoul 110, Korea

U.S. EDITION
First printing 1983
Pace International Research, Inc.
Tide Avenue, Falcon Cove
P.O. Box 51, Arch Cape
Oregon 97102, U.S.A.

ISBN: 0-89209-017-0

This series is a co-publication by ¡The Si-sa-yong-o-sa Publishers, Inc.
and The International Communication Foundation.

Foreword

The Korean people are artistic, expressing their inner-most being in pottery, painting, poetry, drama, music and dance. To most foreigners familiar with Chinese and Japanese art, Korean art comes as a profound revelation and a delightful experience. Korean art differs from the strong, bold aspects of continental Chinese art and from the dazzling colours of Japanese art. Its basic characteristic is simplicity, reinforced by the atmosphere of quiet and serenity which it creates.

Following the publication of *Modern Korean Short Stories*, the Korean National Commission for UNESCO embarked upon a new project, dedicated to seeking real character of Korean culture. This new series deals with various aspects of Korean culture—language, thought, fine arts, music, dance, theatre and cinema, etc. It concentrates on baring the roots of the Korean cultural tradition and demonstrating the process of its transformation. It is hoped in this way to reveal the framework of traditional thought which is fundamental to any understanding of Korea's past and present.

Profound thanks are due to the writers of the individual articles and to the generous sponsorship of the Si-sa-yong-o-sa Publishers, Inc., who once again have turned a dream into a reality. This series, edited by the Korean National Commission for UNESCO, is published by the Si-sa-yong-o-sa Publishers, Inc., in commemoration of the thirtieth anniversary of the Korean National Commission for UNESCO.

Bong Shik Park

Bong Shik Park
Secretary-General
The Korean National Commission
for UNESCO

Contents

Foreword   *v*

Korean Dance Repertories   *1*
Han Man-yŏng

Korean Court Dance   *10*
Sŏng Kyŏng-nin

Korean Traditional Dance   *20*
Kim Ch'ŏn-hŭng, Alan C. Heyman

Reflections on Korean Dance   *31*
Eleanor King

Moving in the Korean Way   *72*
Christine J. Loken

Crane Dances in Korea   *81*
Christine J. Loken

Farmers Music and Dance   *93*
Kim Yang-gon

**Society of Korean Dance Studies Debuts
in West Germany, New York, Honolulu**   *106*
Alan C. Heyman

A Look at the Korean National Ballet   *124*
Christine J. Loken

Contents

History of Korean Theatre, 1908-1945   134
  Yi Tu-hyŏn

Yu Ch'i-jin and the Theatre of Korea   145
  William E. Henthorn

Projection of Tradition in Modern Drama   154
  Yu Min-yŏng

American Drama in Korea, 1945-1970   165
  Yoh Suk-kee

The Cinema in Korea   175
  James Wade

Korea's Film World   195
  James Wade

Contributors in This Volume   205

KOREAN DANCE,
THEATER AND CINEMA

Korean Dance Repertories

HAN MAN-YŎNG

Korean dance may be classified into the following categories: ritual, court, folk and mask.

Ritual Dance

A. *Il-mu* (Line dance; 佾舞)

Il-mu which literally means "line dance," is performed during ritual ceremonies at the Confucian Temple and the Royal Ancestors' Shrine. The suite consists of both a civil and a military dance. The former intends to land the civil virtues of the ancestors while the latter gives tribute to their military conquests and achievements.

A 64-member ensemble of male dancers perform the Confucian Temple ritual dance. During the civil dance, they hold in their right hands a stick with attached pheasant feathers (*chŏk*; 翟) and a flute (*yak*; 籥) in their left.

After the ritual program of the first offering of a libation, the dancers change their attire for the military dance. They carry this time an ax (*ch'ŏk*;戚) in their right hands and a shield (*kan*;干) with their left.

For the Royal Ancestors' Shrine ritual dance, the 36 member ensemble of male dancers line themselves into six columns. The music played is usually slow and symmetrical thus producing gentle body movements. Interestingly enough, though, dynamic movements also pervade the whole atmosphere of the dance.

B. Buddhist Dance (作法)

The Buddhist Dance consists of the Butterfly Dance, the Cymbal Dance, and the Drum Dance. These dances are not particularly spectacular; they are mere offerings of one's body to Buddha. Essential to this kind of dance are the Buddhist chants and instrumental music that set the mood and tone of the dance.

The Butterfly Dance is performed by one or two monks wearing hoods and white costumes to depict butterflies, and holding lotus flowers in their hands. Giving this dance a distinct touch of characterization are its slow, quiet, and somewhat meditative movements, provided by the serene and tranquil tunes of the Buddhist chants.

The Cymbal Dance is performed by four dancers with large cymbals. Loud and noisy songs and the conical oboe, gong, and drum serve as essential features of this dance.

From time to time, the dancers lift the cymbals up above their heads or else strike them.

The Drum Dance is performed by a monk holding drum sticks. Accompanied by loud and uproarious ensemble music, the dancer exuberantly strikes a big drum at random. This beating of the drum signifies Nirvana, that is, "the attainment of salvation" in Buddhist philosophy.

Court Dance

Court Dances were performed at banquets given at the royal court. The court dance takes two forms: *Hyang-ak* and *Tang-ak*. The *Hyang-ak* dance is an indigenous Korean dance dating from far back in ancient times. A characteristic of this dance is an oral preface recited by the dancers in a classical song form.

The best known dances under this category are: *Ch'ŏyong-mu* dance, the Drum Dance, the Crane Dance, the Sword Dance and the Nightingale Dance.

The *Tang-ak* dance, meanwhile, originated from China; but over a long period of time it underwent a process of Koreanization. Thus, we can hardly note any differences in dance movements and accompanying music between *Hyang-ak* and *Tang-ak*. The only thing different is that, in *Tang-ak*, there is a leader holding a long bamboo stick which looks like a broomstick turned upside-down, and who does not dance but recites an oral preface and epilog.

The best known dance under this category is the Ball Throwing Dance.

A. *Hyang-ak Dance* (鄕樂舞)

1. Ch'ŏYONG-MU DANCE (處容舞) — This is a dance of exorcism originating in Kyŏng-ju, in the southeastern part of the Korean peninsula, in the 9th century.

While accompanied by a slow, dignified music *Sujech'ŏn* and *Yŏngsan hoesang*, five male dancers perform wearing masks and attired in costumes of blue, white, red, black and yellow which are symbolic of the east, west, south, north and center of the universe. From time to time, the dancers change positions, make full turns and flap their sleeves as if in flight. Originally, *Ch'ŏyong-mu* was played on New Year's Eve by the lunar calendar as an exorcism ritual.

2. DRUM DANCE (鼓舞) — Eight dancers perform before a big drum. Four of them are the main dancers and hold drum sticks, while the rest are minor performers and hold lotus flowers. As the main dancers beat the drum, the dancers dance around the drum like butterflies flying around a flower.

3. CRANE DANCE (鶴舞) — Two dancers wear crane masks and costumes. They execute movements to express those of the

crane. The cranes approach a big lotus flower and pick it up only to find a little fairy girl in the flower.

4. Sᴡᴏʀᴅ Dᴀɴᴄᴇ (劍舞) — This dance is performed by females in groups, each dancer holding a sword in each hand.

It is based on a legend which tells that in the seventh century, a brave young man of the kingdom of Silla killed an enemy general using the tactic of dancing before him. This act had saved his country from invasion by the enemy forces.

At the opening of the dance, the dancers carry no swords in their hands. They then kneel down and pick up the swords whose short blades are connected to the handles by short wires.

In this way, the swords produce a rattling noise as the dancers brandish them. The metallic sounds provide an inexplicably exotic grace and color to the dance.

Originally masculine and animated, the sword dance gradually transformed itself into a graceful feminine dance. As compared to her East Asian counterparts, the Korean Sword Dance is the only one which does not call for real swordsmanship on the part of the dancer.

5. Nɪɢʜᴛɪɴɢᴀʟᴇ Dᴀɴᴄᴇ (春鶯囀) — This dance is performed solo by a female dancer on a "flower mattress." Clad in a brilliant yellow dress with multi-colored stripes on the sleeves and a flower crown adorning her head, the dancer reveals her exhilarating elegance and beauty by executing graceful and gentle body movements that exhibit her front, side and back, accompanied by the raising of hands or feet.

B. Tang-ak Dance (唐樂舞)

Ball Throwing Dance (抛毬樂) — While executing dancing movements, sixteen women dancers throw a ball through a hole atop a gate. If one misses her face is painted with black ink as a punishment. But if she succeeds, a flower is given to her as a prize.

Folk Dance

Folk Dance, like folk music, expresses the emotions of the people. In contrast to court dance, it reveals a freedom of improvisation without any hint of restraint. The accompanying music is, of course, folk music with a comparatively fast tempo.

The more popular forms of folk dances are: the Farmers' Dance, *Kanggang-suwŏllae*, the Monk's Dance, the Flower-Crown Dance, the Shaman Dance, and *Salp'uri*.

1. FARMERS' DANCE (農樂舞) — This dance is a unique combination of dancing and the rural folk band music, a form of entertainment traditional to the country among the farming folk since the early dawn of history.

This music has such a rousing effect with its complicated rhythms, mostly produced with percussion instruments and a conical oboe, that one cannot suppress a natural swinging motion of the body in pure merriment.

There are numerous forms of this popular kind of dancing. The small hand-drum whirl is performed on a wide field usually by two boy dancers carrying small hand-drums and a long narrow strip of paper stuck on their hats.

To the accompaniment of pompous music, the dancers whirl around with an oblique falling down-like motion, madly beating upon their drums and rotating their heads causing the strips to twirl dazzlingly in the air.

2. KANGGANG-SUWŎLLAE (강강수월래) — The dance accompanying the folk song of *Kanggang-suwŏllae* originated in the southwestern part of Korea. On the night of the full moon of the first and eighth months by the lunar calendar, the maidens of the village gather in an open field to dance around with

joined hands as they sing.

At the start of the dance, the maidens, wearing the ordinary Korean woman's blouse and skirt with long hair tied with ribbons which is a symbol of womanhood, stand in a circle facing the center with joined hands. To the accompaniment of a solo call and choral response in a slow tempo, the dancers move around the circle slowly, quickening their pace everytime as they dance together with the music, and finally, winding up in a whirling climax.

3. MONK'S DANCE (僧舞) — Among the Buddhist dance forms consisting of the Butterfly Dance, the Cymbal Dance, and the Drum Dance, this dance was adopted into the folk dance from the Drum Dance as performed by a professional dancer and came to be known as the Monk's Dance.

The dance is performed in front of a drum. To the accompaniment of music which sounds like the chanting of a Buddhist prayer, the dancer with drumsticks in her hands and dressed in a robe of long sleeves and red *kasa* (a type of cape or mantle worn by Buddhist monks during a ceremony) and a white hood, expresses through body movements the rigors of resisting temptations.

Finally, in the last round of the dance, the dancer strikes the drum displaying the fastest drumming technique, exciting, complicated rhythms in acceleration.

4. FLOWER-CROWN DANCE (花冠舞) — This group dance excites in the viewer a neat, brilliant and colorful feeling owing to the flower crowns atop the dancers' heads plus lotuses in their hands.

5. FAN DANCE (부채춤) — This dance is exuberantly and breath-takingly beautiful. During the entire dance, large fans form variegated patterns, such as butterflies, or a flower in full bloom, or sea waves.

It originated from the shaman dance from which the fan

was adapted. Performing various possible forms in a given space with the fans, it has recently been developed into a magnificent choral dance.

6. SALP'URI (살풀이) — This is perhaps the most fascinating and most complicated of all the folk dances. Danced only by women, it is marked by a delicate line, and improvised movements.

The original intent of *Salp'uri* was exorcism. Here the dancer wears an ordinary Korean woman's blouse and skirt, usually white in color, and carries a long white, silk handkerchief in her right hand.

The dance is accompanied by improvised ensemble music used in the Shaman rite; it expresses a widow's lamentation.

At the climax of the whirling patterns executed by the dancer, the dance come to an abrupt halt.

Mask Dance

This dance is performed in the various mask dance dramas and *Yayu* (野遊) or "field plays", which are played throughout the regions of Korea. These forms of entertainment originated from the morality plays of Buddhism and exorcism. But since then, they have undergone a slow process of transformation and renovation, so that gradually their religious meaning came to be ignored. Today, they are performed merely for entertainment's sake.

The highlights of the dramas and plays are: Old Monk's Dance, Leper Dance, Four Young Buddhist Monks' Dance, Eight Buddhist Monks' Dance and the Lion Dance.

1. THE OLD MONK'S DANCE (老丈춤) — The old monk is dressed in a gray frock and wears a hat made of either moss or fern. Dangling from his neck is a long rosary. He holds a large fan in his right hand, and a long staff in his left.

While he performs slow and gentle movements, he encounters two young sorceresses. Charmed by these two enchanting shamans, the old monk gives his rosary to them. There is a brief moment of silent interruption; the sorceresses hesitate to take the present. However, after a while, the three join together in a dance.

This dance serves as a satire on the apostasy of Buddhist monks.

2. LEPER DANCE (문둥춤) — This dance expresses the grievances and miseries of the leper revealed through the tottering, reeling steps of a dancer wearing a leper's mask.

3. FOUR YOUNG BUDDHIST MONKS' DANCE (四上座춤) — Originally, the dance was performed by males; however, these days, it is more commonly performed by females. The dancers wear Buddhist costumes and white hoods.

Since professional dancers started performing this dance, masks have not been worn anymore. Rather, they freely display their beauteous facial features.

This dance is regarded as the most feminine and most delicate of all the monks' dances. In addition, its technique, charm and quiet movements make it a dance rich in essences and one of highest artistic merit as well.

4. EIGHT BUDDHIST MONKS' DANCE (팔먹중춤) — This dance is perhaps the most vigorous and most masculine of all the Korean mask dances. Performers wear a robe, with longsleeves fully covering their hands, gaily thrust up and down and twirled around in rapid movements. Each monk boasts unabashedly of his special dance prowess.

5. LION DANCE (獅子춤) — One lion is made up of two persons, one in front and the other in the rear. The lion dances around in a large circle, after which he sits down, walks or jumps in the center of the stage, turning his head from left to

right, biting at his body lice, switching his tail, or scratching his body.

In some mask dance plays, there may appear two lions. They face each other and engage in a joyful display of their antics.

Korean Court Dance

Song Kyŏng-nin

The topic Korean court dance, has many aspects. This article will cover some of the major historical changes which have occurred, and then briefly describe *Ch'unaengjŏn* 春鶯囀, one of the most beautiful court dances of Korea.

Korean dance is roughly divided into two types; court dance, which was used in ritual ceremonies and banquets, and folk dance. The court dance which was used in ritual ceremonies is called *Il-mu* 佾舞 ("line dance"), and the dance that was used in banquets, *Chŏng-jae* 呈才 ("showing the talent of dance"). *Il-mu* is quite different from *Chŏng-jae* in its movements, sense, and form.

Il-mu is performed during ritual ceremonies at Confucian Shrines and the Royal Ancestors' Shrine. The suite consists of both a civil and a military dance. The former lauds the civil virtues of the ancestors while the latter pays tribute to their military conquests and achievements.

A 64-member ensemble of male dancers performs the Confucian Shrine ritual dance. During the civil dance, they hold in their right hands a stick with pheasant feathers attached (yak 籥) and a flute (chŏk 翟) in their left.

After the ritual program of the first offering of a libation, the dancers change their attire for the military dance. They carry this time an ax (ch'ŏk 戚) in their right hands and a shield (kan 干) in their left.

For the Royal Ancestors' Shrine ritual dance, the 36-member ensemble of male dancers line themselves into six columns. The music played is usually slow and symmetrical thus producing gentle body movements. Interestingly enough dynamic movements also pervade the whole atmosphere of the dance.

Chŏng-jae is the name used for dance combined with song, and it literally means showing the talent of the dancer to the king.

Unified Silla (669-935)

In the Silla period a Ministry of Music 音聲署 was established to perform royal ceremonies, banquets and ritual ceremonies. At this time musicians were sent to T'ang 唐 China to learn Chinese music and dance, and Chinese musical instruments, dance costumes and stage properties were imported. In this way, the music and dance of Silla were influenced by Chinese culture.

During that period, dances of Central Asian origin such as the Lion Dance, an acrobatic ball-juggling dance, and mask dances, were also performed, and were called Korean dance. This means that they had already been Koreanized.

Other *Hyang-ak* (Korean) dances of that period which still survive are *Ch'ŏyong-mu* 處容舞 and the sword dance (*Kŏm-mu* 劍舞).

		Chug-ganja[1]	Kuho[2]	Ch'iŏ[3]	Ch'ang-sa[4]	entrance[5]	exit[5]
Chinese style	Suyŏnjang	2	2		2	dancing	dancing
	Yŏnhwadae	2	2		3	enter and dance	bow twice
	Oyangsŏn	2	2	2	2	enter with *chokto*[6]	dancing
	P'ogurak	2	2		16	dancing	dancing
	Hŏnsŏndo	2	2		7	dancing	dancing
Korean style	Tongdong				1	enter, *chokto* and bow	bow and exit
	Mugo				1	enter and bow to the north	bow and exit
	Muae				1	enter, *chokto* and bow	bow and exit

1. A *Chugganja* 竹竿子 is an usher with a bamboo stick ten feet long, who leads the dancers onto the dancing area. Two *Chug-ganjas* are needed in a Chinese style court dance (*Tang-ak Chŏng-jae*).
2. A *Kuho* 口號 is a classical chant performed by the *Chugganja*. In a *Tang-ak* dance, the *Kuho* is performed twice, once at the beginning and once at the end of the dance. It is a narration about the theme of the dance to be performed, and a prayer for long life for the king and a peaceful world.
3. A *Ch'iŏ* 致語 is a chant or a poem recited for long life for the king and a peaceful world. It is chanted by the *Chugganja* in the middle of the dance and used only in *Tang-ak* dances.
4. A *Ch'angsa* 唱詞 is a classical song sung by the dancers. It is used in both *Tang-ak* and *Hyang-ak* dances. The text of the song is a poem written in Chinese in *Tang-ak* dance, while a poem written in Korean is used in a *Hyang-ak* dance.
5. Entrance onto the dance area and exit. In *Tang-ak* dance, the dancers are led by two *Chugganjas*, or ushers. When the *Chug-ganjas* enter the dance area, they chant an announcement of the theme of the dance about to be performed (*Kuho*). Then, the dancers enter dancing. When the dance is finished, the *Chuggan-jas* also chant another *Kuho* for long life for the king and exit, and the dancers follow. *Yŏnhwadae* is an exception. It is performed as a *Hyang-ak* dance.

    In a *Hyang-ak* dance there is no *Chugganja* and the dancers walk out onto the dance area and take up position with their heads bent to hide their faces with their colorful sleeves. When the music begins, the dancers bow to the king who is sitting to the north. They also sing a *Ch'angsa* in the middle of the dance. When they finish the dance, they bow against to the king and exit.
6. A *Chokto* 足蹈 is the preparatory movement with which the dancers take up their positions.

Koryŏ Period (918-1392)

In the music section of the *History of Koryŏ* 高麗史樂志,

eight dances are listed with some explanations.

A. Chinese style court dance (*Tang-ak* dance)

   1. *Hŏnsŏndo* 獻仙桃 : the dance of presenting the peach from fairy land

   2. *Suyŏnjang* 壽延長 : a prayer dance for long life for the king

   3. *Oyangsŏn* 五羊仙 : the dance of five fairies

   4. *P'ogurak* 抛毬樂 : the ball playing dance

   5. *Yŏnhwadae* 蓮花臺 : the dance of the lotus flower

B. Korean style court dance (*Hyang-ak* dance)

   6. *Mugo* 舞鼓 : drum dance

   7. *Tongdong* 動動 : castanets dance

   8. *Muae* 無㝵 : calabash dance

Early Yi Dynasty Period (1393-1800)

Nineteen dances are listed in the *Akhak kwebŏm* 樂學軌範, "The Treatise on Music" compiled in 1493.

A. *Tang-ak* dance

   1. *Kokp'a* 曲破 : the grand dance

   2. *Kŭnch'ŏnjŏng* 勤天庭 : the dance in praise of the civil virtue of the founding king of Yi dynasty

   3. *Kŭmch'ŏk* 金尺 : the dance of a golden measure

   4. *Sŏngt'aek* 聖澤 : the dance celebrating the king's benevolence

   5. *Sumyŏngmyŏng* 受明命 : the dance for the founding king of Yi dynasty receiving Heaven's decree

   6. *Suborok* 受寶籙 : the dance for the founding king of Yi dynasty receiving Heaven's holy scripture

   7. *Suyŏnjang* 壽延長 : the prayer dance for long life for the king

   8. *Yŏnhwadae* 蓮花臺 : the dance of the lotus flower

   9. *Oyangsŏn* 五羊仙 : the dance of the five fairies

   10. *Yukhwadae* 六花隊 : the six flower dance

   11. *P'ogurak* 抛毬樂 : the ball playing dance

12. *Hasŏngmyŏng* 賀聖明 : the dance celebrating the king's reign
13. *Hahwangŭn* 賀皇恩 : the dance celebrating the king's benevolence
14. *Hŏnsŏndo* 獻仙桃 : the dance presenting the peach from fairyland to the king or queen

B. *Hyang-ak* dance

15. *Mugo* 舞鼓 : the drum dance
16. *Mundŏkkok* 文德曲 : the dance praising the founding king of Yi dynasty for his civil virtue
17. *Pongnaeŭi* 鳳來儀 : the dance to the poem "The Flying Dragon"
18. *Abak* 牙拍 : the ivory clapper dance
19. *Muae* 無㝵 : the calabash dance

Tang-ak dance	Chugganja	Kuho	Ch'iŏ	Ch'angsa	entrance	exit
1*	2	2		2	dancing	dancing
2	2	2	1	1	dancing	dancing waving the sleev
3	2	2	1	3	dancing with flowers	same as above
4	2	2	1	1	dancing	same as above
5	2	2	1	1	dancing with flowers	same as above
6	2	2	1	1	dancing	dancing
7	2	2		3	dancing with flowers	dancing waving the sleev
8	2	2		1	dancing	no exit
9	2	2		3	dancing	dancing waving the sleev
10	2	2	2	7	dancing	same as above
11	2	2		18	dancing with flowers	same as above
12	2	2	1	1	same as above	same as above
13	2	2	1	1	same as above	same as above
14	2	2	1	8	same as above	same as above

Hyang-ak dance	Chugganja	Kuho	Ch'iŏ	Ch'angsa	entrance	exit
15				1	enter, sit and bow	bow and dancing
16			1	4	dancing	dancing
17	2	2		28	dancing with flowers	dancing waving the sleev
18				3	dancing and bow	bow and dancing
19				1	enter and dance	same as above

*The numbers are the name of the dance.

1. The *Kuho* was performed twice by the *Chugganja*, once at the beginning and once at the end of a *Tang-ak* dance as in the Koryŏ period. However, in a *Hyang-ak* dance, there was no *Chugganja*, (except in the dance *Pongnaeŭi*), and no *Kuho* was chanted.
2. The *Ch'iŏ* was usually chanted by the primadonna of the *Tang-ak* dance, but in the seven dances — *Kŭmch'ok*, *Suborok*, *Kŭnch'ŏn-jŏng*, *Sumyŏngmyŏng*, *Hahwang'ŭn*, *Hasŏngcho*, *Sŏngt'aek* — which praise the founding king's achievements of Yi dynasty, the *Chokcha* |簇子|(ten-foot-tall, flag-like prop) holder chanted the *Ch'iŏ*.
3. The *Ch'angsa* was a poem written in Chinese in the *Tang-ak* dance, and a poem written in Korean in the *Hyang-ak* dance.
4. Entrance and exit onto the dance area. In *Tang-ak* dances the dancers entered dancing as in the Koryŏ period, but they exited waving their sleeves.

   The *Hyang-ak* dance was performed just as in the Koryŏ period with the dance beginning with the dancers in set position on the stage.

Accompanying Music

Tang-ak was mainly used for the *Tang-ak* dances. *Pohŏja* was the most favored music for the dances. *Hyang-ak* accompanied the *Hyang-ak* dance. For example,

Dance	Accompanied music
Pongnae'ŭi	*Yŏmillak* composed by King Sejong
Ivory clapper dance(*Abak*)	*Tongdong*
Drum dance (*Mugo*)	*Chŏngŭp*
Cymbal dance (*Hyangbal*)	*Hyang-dang Kyoju*
Crane dance (*Hak-mu*)	*Pohŏja*

* The crane dance is exceptional, in that it used a *Tang-ak* piece, *Pohŏja*.

Late Yi Dynasty (since 19th century)

The two years of 1828 and 1829 could be marked as epoch-making in the history of Korean dance. Prince Ikchong 翼宗, an excellent dancer and choreographer, made 23 new pieces. They were:

1. *Kainjŏn moran* 佳人剪牧丹 : a beauty picks a peony
2. *Kyŏngp'ung-do* 慶豊圖 : scene of celebration
3. *Koguryŏ-mu* 高句麗舞 :dance of Koguryŏ
4. *Kongmak-mu* 公莫舞 : sword dance
5. *Mansu-mu* 萬壽舞 : the prayer dance for long life for the king
6. *Mangsŏnmun* 望仙門 : the dance with large fans (ten-foot-tall, flag-like fan)
7. *Musanhyang* 舞山香 : the solo dance around a tortoise-shell
8. *Pakch'ŏp-mu* 撲蝶舞 : butterfly dance
9. *Posang-mu* 寶相舞 : ball playing dance
10. *Simhyangch'un* 沈香春 : flower dance
11. *Yŏnhwa-mu* 蓮花舞 : the dance of the lotus flower
12. *Yŏngji-mu* 影池舞 : the dance around the pond
13. *Ch'ŏpsŭng-mu* 疊勝舞 : the dance in celebration of a peaceful world
14. *Ch'oehwa-mu* 崔花舞 : the dance in celebration of the flowery spring
15. *Ch'un'gwangho* 春光好 : the dance in celebration of spring
16. *Ch'undae okch'ok* 春坮玉燭 : spinning dance
17. *Ch'unaengjŏn* 春鶯囀 : the dance of the nightingale singing in springtime
18. *Hyangnyŏng-mu* 響鈴舞 : the dance with small bells
19. *Hŏnch'ŏnhwa* 獻天花 : five fairies dedicate heavenly flowers to the king
20. *Sasŏn-mu* 四仙舞 : the dance of four fairies
21. *Yŏnpaekbokchi-mu* 演百福之舞 : the dance in praise of the king's virtue

22. *Changsaeng poyŏnji-mu* 長生寶宴之舞： the dance in celebration of a peaceful world and banquet
23. *Chesuch'ang* 帝壽昌： the dance in praise of the king's reign

The above 23 dances lost any distinction of *Tang-ak* and *Hyang-ak* styles, in which the dancers entered and exited dancing whether they had a *Chugganja* or not, and *Ch'angsa* poems written in Chinese were sung.

Beginning in the 19th century, every court dance had its own opening arrangement for the dancers. When the dance was over, the dancers returned to their opening positions, and then retreated. The dancers did not bow to the king any more. This indicates that the court ceremony was no longer the ruling influence in the presentation of dances but that artistic considerations were gaining in importance.

Ch'unaengjŏn 春鶯囀

Ch'unaengjŏn, or "Nightingale Singing in Springtime" was danced at royal banquets and is regarded as one of the representative dances of Korea together with *Ch'ŏyong-mu* 處容舞 . It is danced on a "flower mattress", a straw woven mat. This unique solo dance was performed by a female dancer clad in a brilliant yellow cloak with multi-colored stripes on the sleeves and a flower crown adorning her head.

After some short introductory movements, the dancer sings the *Ch'angsa:*

A beauty strolls under the bright moon. 娉婷月下步
A breeze moves colorful sleeves lightly. 羅袖舞風輕
With the most beautiful movement, Hwajŏnt'ae,
I appeal to the King's love. 君王任多情

The dance is performed to the accompaniment *P'yŏngjo*

hoesang. It begins very slowly and moves slowly through 5 rhythmic changes, each becoming progressively faster. The dancer begins by standing at the far end of the rectangular mat facing the king who sits to the north. To the rhythmic pattern of *Sang-yŏngsan* 上靈山, with a slow twenty-beat measure, she progresses down the mat in the introductory walk or *Yŏmsu chokto* 斂手足蹈. During this introductory walk, her hands inside the gaily colored *hansam* 汗衫 sleeves meet and lie gently on her skirt. As she reaches the front edge her hands come up before her face, and we hear the sound of the clapper, *pak* 拍, just before she sings the *Ch'angsa* as written above.

After the song, the clapper sounds again and the rhythm changes to *Se-ryŏngsan* 細靈山 (the third of the eight pieces of *P'yŏngjo hoesang*), with a somewhat lighter ten-beat measure. At the beginning of this section, the dancer's arms are raised above her head and then to the new rhythm she steps first to the right and then left with the same arm describing a large half circle in the air as it moves down to her side and back into position above her head. Then with arms outstretched the dancer walks in small circles first to the right and then to the left, at the end of which the *pak* again sounds and the rhythm changes. At this point the rhythm heard is *Yŏmbul todŭri* (the sixth piece of the suite), a six-beat measure with a strong feel to it.

To this *todŭri* rhythm the dancer sways and stretches gently forward and back, first with arms outstretched and then with the hands touching and lying on her skirt. The emphasis in this section as in those before is on the heavy quality of her movements and the grace with which she rides the waves of her breath and body movements. The light quality of her long sleeves provides an effective contrast with the heavy quality of her skirt and the slow solemn quality of the music and her movements. She does indeed seem to personify the soaring quality of a nightingale, yet she is confined to the narrow space of one mat. She walks forward, again with the traditional rolling gait and raises her arms as the clapper signals yet another change in the rhythm.

The new rhythmic pattern, a fast *Yŏmbul*, is still in a six-beat measure but is exactly twice the speed of the previous rhythmic pattern. Here the dancer may display a slightly coquettish attitude (*Hwajŏnt'ae* 花前態) and perhaps even a smile as she steps gently in pace and then backs up the length of the mat.

Then the clapper sounds again and the rhythmic pattern changes to the final piece, *T'aryŏng* 打令, a rolling beat with four sets of triplets per measure. To this rhythm the dancer moves down the mat with outstretched arms again turning to the right and then the left. With great swooping movements of her arms she sways forward and back with a slight complimentary twist in her torso and then proceeds down the mat passing her arms gently over her head from side to side. With a great circle of her arms she brings them down and places them behind her back as she sweeps in place again and with arms outstretched executes a slow turn to the left followed by two faster ones. Then with arms outstreched she backs up the mat to the far end and ends the dance with a slow bow.

Korean Traditional Dance

The Chinju Sword Dance
and the T'ongyŏng Sŭngjŏn-mu

KIM CH'ŎN-HŬNG
WITH ALAN C. HEYMAN

Korean traditional dance can be divided into two categories with regard to its process of development. One is court dance, which was performed at court festivities and banquets for the royal family and at receptions for foreign emissaries. The heritage of court dance style and costume differs considerably from that of the folk.

The other category of dance is that which was performed at private parties held by the ruling upper class aristocracy. This dance was performed by professional female entertainers known as *kisaeng* (the Korean counterpart of the Japanese *geisha*) who were officially designated as regular entertainers. This dance form, which originated in the court, underwent changes in form and custom in its adaptation to the environment outside the palace. Here, the dance costume retains some points from that of its original form, the court dance, combined with that worn everyday by the common people. And, moreover, as the dance found its way further into each particular region of the country, it was affected by such factors as time and motivation in accordance with the locale in which it settled down. These dances, which retained a facsimile of the form and content of the court dance, were particularly influenced by local color, into which all factors were combined.

However, the dances which sprang originally from each native region of the country must be considered under a separate category, as their form and content were totally different from those of the court.

Two traditional dances representative of the second category mentioned above are the "Sword Dance *(Kŏm-mu)*" from the Chinju area (South Kyŏngsang Province) and the "Dance of Victory *(Sŭngjŏn-mu)*" from the T'ongyŏng (Ch'ungmu) region, also located in South Kyŏngsang Province.

Sword Dance

As this particular sword dance differs from that which was performed at court, it is given the specific title of "Chinju Sword Dance."

In comparison with the sword dance of the court, the Chinju version contains more variety in the rhythm of the accompanying music, and in the latter part one finds more active movements performed in time with a rapid tempo. However, the dance is quite different from the folk dance in general in both character and usage, wherein it more closely resembles the court dance form.

Of all Korean traditional dances, the Chinju Sword Dance boasts the longest history and the most unique form.

Origin of the Sword Dance

During the Three kingdoms period, when the kingdoms of Silla and Paekche were at war, it was learned that a *hwarang*, a young knight, had fought bravely and sacrificed his life for his country. In praise of his heroic action, the people of Silla thereafter performed a dance wearing a mask made in the likeness of the *hwarang*'s face while they wielded a sword. From that time onward until the succeeding Koryŏ period, the dance was favored by the commoners, but it was not performed at court. However, with the passing of time, the dance underwent some changes in that the mask was gradually discarded and the dance came to be performed by two or more persons in ensemble.

Comparatively late in the succeeding Yi dynasty, the sword dance found its way into the court dance répertoire. There it was performed by four female court dancers, two on each side facing each other, in which each participant, brandishing the swords with wide inward and outward motion of the arms, pretended to do battle with the dancer on the opposing side.

From the beginning of the 19th century, after the sword dance was introduced to the Chinju region by the officially designated *kisaeng* of the Chinju district, the form of the court sword dance and that of the Chinju area became different, and these differences were to be maintained through succeeding generations. The Chinju Sword Dance was performed at large banquets and festivities held in the Chinju area.

The Form of the Sword Dance

The dancers wear the ordinary Korean woman's blouse and skirt over which they don a type of frock that was worn by the military in ancient times, called a *chŏnbok*, and a deep blue sash, called a *chŏndae*, which is tied around the waist. The hat which is worn is also derived from ancient military attire and is called a *chŏllip* (battle hat). The dancers' hands are covered completely by long, brightly rainbow-colored sleeves, consisting of nine colors in all, which are worn around the wrists.

At the start of the dance, four dancers take the center of the stage and face each other, two on each side.

To the tempo of a slow 6/4-beat rhythm, called *yŏmbul*

(literally, "Buddhist invocation"), the dancers' arms are raised slowly, and outstretched, and each dancer moves toward the other and then retreats to the original position. Each step requires three beats of the 6/4 rhythmic meter, a pattern which is quite similar to that of the court dance.

When the rhythm changes to *t'aryŏng*, a 12/8 meter with the accent falling on the ninth beat, the dance movement, following the rhythm, is slightly accelerated. Here, each step requires two beats of the 12/8 meter. The dancers, once again facing each other, move toward one another. When they reach the point where they are almost touching each other, they execute a slight backward motion and bend the head backwards so that the face is looking straight upward. Then each dancer places her hands upon the other's shoulders and moves her body slightly to the right and left with subtle and graceful motion. Then, once again, they slowly move away from each other, retreating backwards to the original starting point, always keeping in time, of course, with the accompanying rhythm.

After repeating the above-mentioned patterns two or three times, the sleeves are removed from the hands and placed outside the performing area. The dance then continues with the performers facing offstage and performing a series of dance movements in a standing position called *ipch'um-sawi* ("standing dance" movement), followed by another movement, called *pangsŏk-tori* ("turning on a cushion"), wherein the dancers squat on a cushion, or mat, placed on the floor, and turn around until they are facing each other. These two movements, the *ipch'um-sawi* and the *pangsŏk-tori*, are repeated in alternation, after which the accompanying music is accelerated to a faster *t'aryŏng* tempo and the dance movement follows suit.

In time with the music and accelerated tempo, two of the dancers, moving in the direction of stage-center, wave their hands back and forth in a type of curving, undulating motion that is intended to simulate the brandishing of the swords. No swords, however, are present at this time in the hands of these two dancers. At this point, the two remaining dancers, holding a sword in each hand, appear and place the swords in front of the two dancers at stage-center, after which they exit. The two dancers at stage-center then, facing each other, come to a kneeling position before the swords and, lowering the hands gradually in the same swaying, undulating motion, until they reach the place where the swords are lying, very gracefully and softly caress the top and sides of the swords. After this, they grasp the two front tails of the frock — the military garb called the *ch'ŏnbok* — and tie the ends in a knot behind them. This might be interpreted as a preparation for the commencement of combat.

The first sword is picked up in the right hand of the dancer and waved to the right and left several times, after which the left hand follows suit. This action is then repeated by both hands simultaneously until the two swords are brought toward the center of the body and tucked under the armpits, blades facing inward. Once this is accomplished, the accompanying rhythm returns once again to the original *t'aryŏng* pattern.

The *t'aryŏng* here, however, is played even slower than that called for by the original pattern, and the two dancers, after slowly rising to a standing position, dance and manipulate the swords in a very mild and graceful manner until they have each moved to the position formerly occupied by the other, whereupon they once again return to their original places.

Once this is accomplished, the *t'aryŏng* once again returns to the accelerated tempo executed previously and the dancers wield the swords in the same manner executed at the beginning, the dance also gradually accelerating in tempo.

Thus, the two dancers, brandishing the swords, facing each other and moving toward and away from one another, enter into a section of the dance known as *yunp'ung-dae* that highlights the singularity of the Chinju Sword Dance.

There are four types of *yunp'ung-dae* in the Chinju Sword Dance. The first is executed with the swords tucked under the armpits, as mentioned previously, while the dancers move around in a large complete circle until returning to their original starting points. The second is executed with the tips of the blade touching the left and right side of the dancers' hips. The third is executed brandishing the two swords in a waving motion, as was done previously. The fourth is executed with the left sword tucked under the left armpit and the right sword brandished in a waving motion.

While executing the *yunp'ung-dae*, one foot is extended forward while the entire body is quickly hunched forward in a tight grip and then raised back upwards, whereupon a deep backbend is executed with the back and hips extended far forward so that the head finally comes to rest on the place between the calf and the thigh, directly posterior to the kneecap. This particular movement, which is executed by the dancers moving in a large complete circle, calls for a very rapid motion; if done otherwise, the dancer is apt to lose her balance and fall.

After this movement is concluded, the four dancers line up on the stage and face the audience. They raise their arms above their heads and continue waving the swords. They then move to stage-front and execute a special type of bow that is only to be found in the Sword Dance.* The dance is thus concluded.

The "Chinju Sword Dance" may be regarded as a most gracious and beautiful dance whose movements are executed with soft and subtle motions throughout. It is entirely lacking anything that may be considered brusque or distasteful.

Sŭngjŏn-mu**

This dance is also known as *"T'ongyŏng Puk-ch'um"* (The

---

*The bow is executed thus: the dancer kneels on one foot and brings both swords forward slowly in a very gradual descent until both tips are touching the stage.
** *mu* means dance.

Drum Dance of T'ongyŏng, T'ongyŏng being the name of a town in South Kyŏngsang Province). This dance is quite similar to the *Mu-go* (Drum Dance) of the court in that the color of the costumes of the *wŏn-mu*, the principal dancers in this particular case, and the properties used, such as the large round drum placed in the center of the stage or performance area, and the drumsticks, are also quite similar. Also, as in the court drum dance, the *wŏn-mu* consist of four dancers who dance around the outer circumference of the large drum.

However, the difference between the two dances lies in the fact that in the court drum dance, the *wŏn-mu* and the secondary dancers *(hyŏp-mu)* perform together in ensemble, whereas in the *Sŭngjŏn-mu*, the *hyŏp-mu* only sing and do not dance***

Origin of the Dance

Toward the end of the Koryŏ kingdom, at about the beginning of the 14th century, a civil courtier**** named Yi Hŏn was exiled to a place called Yŏnghae. By chance, as he was strolling along the seashore, he spied a huge raft made of enormous logs floating on the sea. From the huge log he made a very large drum which, when struck, it is said, emitted a thunderous sound that inspired people to dance, and gave birth eventually to the creation of the *Mu-go*, the "Drum Dance," which was later adopted into the court dance répertoire of the Koryŏ and succeeding Yi dynasties.

During the Hideyoshi Invasion of Korea by Japan (end of the 16th century), an admiral by the name of Yi Sun-sin dwelled in the district of T'ongyŏng, a town located in South Kyŏngsang Province. In order to elevate the morale of the men

*** It should be noted here that in the *Mu-go* the *wŏn-mu* make up the inner circle of dancers the *hyŏp-mu* the outer circle, the dancers thus assuming a different role than that of their counterparts in the *Sŭngjŏn-mu*. Another difference lies in the fact that the contents of the songs *(ch'ang-sa)* sung during the *Mu-go* and the *Sŭngjŏn-mu* differ.

**** Courtiers were divided into two categories, civil and military.

under his command, he ordered that the official female entertainers *(kisaeng)* of the T'ongyŏng district perform a dance. The dance performed was the *Mu-go* of the court, but the dance form and the contents of the accompanying song *(ch'ang-sa)* were altered. That is, the dance became a paean to the loyalty and moral spirit of Admiral Yi and therefore underwent changes accordingly, as did the contents of the accompanying song, the *ch'ang-sa*, which became a supplication for victory and a song of felicitation when that victory was achieved.

From its inception onward, the dance was often performed following a military victory as a dance of celebration and every year thenceforth after the death of Admiral Yi, as a dance of dedication, performed at the memorial ceremonies commemorating the day of his death *(Ch'unch'uhyŏng-gi)* and his birth *(T'ansin-je)*, held at his memorial shrine.

It is for this reason that the dance took on the title of *Sŭngjŏn-mu* (Dance of Victory); that is, to celebrate Admiral Yi Sun-sin's great naval victory over the Japanese during the Hideyoshi Invasion.

This dance was handed down to succeeding generations by the *kisaeng* of the Chinju district, mentioned in the previous section on the "Sword Dance." Recently, however, it is performed by young girls residing in the T'ongyŏng area.

The Form of the Dance

A very large round drum is placed stage-center, or in the center of the performing area, and in front of it are placed four pairs of long drumsticks.

The *wŏn-mu*, consisting of four persons, each wears a frock over the customary (Korean style) skirt and blouse that is composed, respectively, of red, blue, black and white-colored materials. Their hands are covered by rainbow-colored sleeves that comprise a total of nine different colors, and on their heads they wear a small gaily-ornamented crown that is called a *hwa-gwan* (flower-crown), adorned with tiny trinkets that quiver and shimmer with even the slightest movement of the dancer. The *hyŏp-mu,* also consisting of four persons, wear ordinary dress; that is, plain white.

To the accompaniment of a very slow *todūri* (six-beat) rhythm (the rhythm is standard *todūri* but the melody differs from that which is usually played), the four *wŏn-mu* enter the stage in a line until they reach stage-center where the large drum and sticks are located. They then turn and face the audience. The dance then commences. At the start, each dancer slowly raises one arm until it reaches the shoulder level and is almost touching the hand of the adjacent dancer. That is, one dancer raises the right arm and the other the left, pairing off the four dancers into two with fingertips almost touching. The dancers then bring both their arms down in front of them abruptly and bring the hands close together.

They then seat themselves slowly and quietly before the drumsticks. Each arm is then abruptly brought upward in an alternate motion, and then downward to where the drumsticks lie. Their hands then hover over the drumsticks and are moved as if they seem to be caressing the sticks. The right and left arms are then alternately waved up and down and brought into an undulating, swaying motion in front of the body. The drumsticks are then picked up and placed inside the colored sleeves and the dancers slowly rise and begin to dance around the large drum until each one has stationed herself at one of the four opposite ends of the drum. Thus, as it turns out, the dancer who is standing directly in front of the drum at stage-center is wearing the blue frock, which represents North, the one who wears the red frock is to the right of the drum, which is East, the black-frocked dancer on the left symbolizes West, and finally, to the rear of the drum at the point furthest from the audience, stands the dancer dressed in white, representing South. In the meantime, the four *hyŏp-mu* have stationed themselves in an outer circle around the *wŏn-mu* so that each one is standing in a position located between each of the *wŏn-mu.*

The *wŏn-mu* then begin to dance around slowly in their respective positions and then move in toward the drum and away from it. Following this, each moves around the drum in a counter-clockwise direction until they have once again reached their original positions. The music then stops and the *hyŏp-mu* sing a song known as a *ch'ang-sa*, while the *wŏn-mu* move once again in a counterclockwise direction, as was done previously. Following the conclusion of the *ch'ang-sa*, the accompanying music plays *t'aryŏng*, a rhythmetic pattern consisting of 12 beats with the accent on the ninth. The *wŏn-mu* then beat the large drum and dance in time with the *t'aryŏng* rhythm. They then raise both arms very high above the head and bring the sticks down on the drum, giving off a resounding "boom," whereupon they turn in their respective positions and move in a counter-clockwise direction to the next point, where the same motion is repeated. They then continue to repeat the same at all four points until the circle has been completed.

Following this, the *ch'ang-sa* is accelerated and the large drum is struck, this time with only one hand while the other is waved in a circular motion around the head. Each dancer then turns around in her respective position and moves on to the next point in a counter-clockwise direction, as was done previously, where the same motion is repeated. The dancers then continue to do the same at each point around the drum, all the while continuing to accelerate the song and dance at an ever more rapid pace.

At the conclusion of the dance, the four *wŏn-mu* line up in front of the drum and face the audience, as was done at the very outset. They then raise both arms high above the head and bring their sleeves down abruptly in front of them. Then, bringing their hands together, they slowly come to a sitting position and execute a bow. Rising once again, they bow out, moving to the rear and finally off-stage.

The *ch'ang-sa* sung by the *hyŏp-mu* during this dance is

translated as follows:

"The moon is rising high, ever so gently,
*Chi-hwa, chi-hwa, chi-hwa-ja,** *
*Uh-gi-ya, uh-ga, uh-huh-jum,*** *
Chi-hwa, chi-hwa, chi-hwa-ja,

*By the favor of our illustrious admiral of Ch'ung mu,**** *
Chi-hwa, chi-hwa, chi-hwa-ja,
*Today is a day of great rejoicing,***** *
Chi-hwa, chi-hwa, chi-hwa-ja."

---

*A chorus of nonsense syllables sung by dancers for the purpose of keeping time with the rhythm
**A chorus of nonsense syllables sung by boatmen as they ply the oars in time with the rhythm of the song
***Ch'ungmu is another name for T'ongyŏng, where Admiral Yi resided
****Sung in celebration of a victory

Reflections on Korean Dance

ELEANOR KING

Observing Asian dance in general, the Western dancer looks immediately to its first great distinction. Dance of sacred character with ancient tradition is irresistable to us of the West who have nothing comparable, except for the American Indian dance heritage, and the Indians of course, originated in Asia in the first place. With us dance is a secular amusement, an entertainment; not central, only peripheral to the culture.

In this respect, then, as a somewhat culturally-deprived American dancer, I look to the East with admiration and rejoice that I have been privileged to see many kinds of 'divine dancing' in Korea. My view is necessarily limited, based on a three-month Fulbright Research grant last fall, with an additional four months this spring, ending in June — obviously only time enough to glimpse the surface of a large and complex field. And I am speaking only as a professionally trained, non-academic dancer, an incurable amateur, who looks at Korean dance with lenses colored by brief exposures to a few other Asian forms: four study periods in Japan, two visits to Thailand; one each to Bali,[1] Sri Lanka, Burma and Taiwan.

In my pursuit of what one Japanese professional calls 'the finest dancing in Asia,'[2] I have been greatly helped by Dr. Yi Tu-hyŏn, of Seoul National University, for his invaluable aid; to Clark Sorenson, Laurel Kendall, Ellen Unruh and Dr. Yun Sun-Yŏng of Ewha Womans University, fellow-Fulbrighters, for assistance in observing Shaman Dance here in Seoul and in the provinces. Printed sources are Alan C.

Heyman's valuable "Dances of The Three Thousand League Land,"[3] and the many articles on Shamanism in the *Korea Journal*. I am grateful to Pak Sang-wan for helping me with his translations and interpretations to see through Korean eyes. Dr. Kim Ki-su, director of the Korea National Classical Music Institute, extended the rare privilege of a special performance of traditional music and dance at the small National Theater. For the experience of dancing Korean classical dances I am grateful to Kim Mae-ja, Yi Ae-ju and Mun Il-ji admired and respected teachers. To them and all the other professional as well as folk-artists, the dancing shamans and Buddhist monks whom I have seen, deep thanks for thus widening my horizons.

Korea's six varieties of traditional dance include: shaman, Buddhist and Confucian rituals; court entertainments; country or folk dances; and the mask-dance drama. The characteristic Korean movements are the heel walk, and turning on the heels; raising the body softly and lightly from bent knee position; slight vibrations from the hips up; the pulses from the shoulders; economy of movement, and improvisation. The most distinctive of Korean movements is the suspended position, balancing on one foot with the free leg extended while the shoulders softly rise and fall. With its élan, this expression conveys a deep sense of ecstatic power. Ecstasy permeates all of the types of dance — not only the shaman and farmers folk dance, but even the extremely formal limited court dance has shoulder pulsations — actually from the chest, in breath rhythm — indicating that secret inner joy of motion which we call Dionysian. Compared to the decorative restrained Japanese dances with their tightly controlled formalism, which I like to consider indicative of the Apollonian order, it seems to me that the soul of Korea as revealed in their dances, proclaims them to be the Dionysians of East Asia.

Korean expression — as is true of Asian dance in general, differs from the West. We explicit the personality, the sex, the body of the dancer; the Korean dancer is impersonal, sexuality suppressed. We like to dominate space and play with light, sound, texture and dynamics for their sensational qualities. The Korean dancer is not interested in external aspects of acrobatic physical motion but rather in expressing metaphysical joy... *mŏt* and *hŭng*. Where we stress nudity, the Korean body, concealed in voluminous silks, with full sleeves, becomes the image of some idealized flower or bird inhabiting a pure and abstract landscape, reflecting several thousand years of influence from surrounding cultures modified by innate sophisticated taste.

Ceremonial Dance

Dance in its origin is sacred, magical and ritual in character. Of Korea's three ritual forms: shaman, Buddhist, and Confucian, we begin with the last and will end with the first, for Shamanism is the most highly developed of all and pervades all of the others, while with Confucianism, where the dancing is minimal, the ceremony is all. Twice a year at Sŏng Kyun Kwan University on the sage's birthday September 2, and on March 21, eight rows of eight students honor Confucius with several other Chinese and Korean scholars, by rhythmically bowing left, right and center. In the first part they hold a flute in one hand and a dragon-headed stick in the other; in the second half they beat wooden hammers on wooden shields. Graded rows of jadeite stone gongs, and bronze bells are part of the extraordinary antique musical accompaniment for the reverent slow-motion bowing, the ritualized incantation of poems and the libations of 'divine wine.' No one is so impolite as to walk down the center path, which is left free to welcome the spirits. No such ceremony exists in China; Korea alone preserves this celebration.[4] For the first time in its long history in the spring of '77, all the student performers were women. We can only guess what

Confucius would think of this innovation, performed two thousand five hundred and eighty one other times by men only.

Attending this year's grand ceremony at the Chongmyo (Royal Family Shrine) May First, when reverence is paid to the spirits of some twenty Yi dynasty kings and queens, we heard the music and saw the dance which is designated Intangible National Cultural Property No. 1 by the Korean government. Court dignitaries make an imposing spectacle officiating before the twenty individual shrines, and the special music, composed by King Sejong, using the same graded-by-thickness jade-stone gongs, bells and other ancient instruments, has a richer texture than for the Confucian rites. The *Il-mu* (lit. line dance), again for eight rows of eight and again women students, in purple-lined cerise robes and courtier hats, is a little more elaborate. They go so far as to circle their arms and forearms, and bending one knee, lift the other leg from the ground three times, in addition to repeated bows facing the shrine, the west and the east. This was introduced to Korea from the Sung dynasty, China, 1114 A.D. Performed in slow-motion, one feels sacral reverence for the ancestral spirits.

Confucian influence on the dance has been mainly repressive, but Buddhism—with a permissive attitude—has contributed a positive influence, as some of the most beautiful court dances and many shaman rituals, especially those for the dead, show.

Court Dance

Korea's court dance has ancient roots. Four hundred years before the emergence of Western renaissance court ballets in Italy, in the middle Koryŏ period (11th century), the women court performers created elaborate poetic spectacles, which had sung verses as prelude and postlude, symbolic properties, magnificent costumes and special music. The boating dance, for example, with thirty-two maidens dancing, had six who pulled a boat with two children aboard. After dropping anchor, the craft was made to circle, pulled with ropes by four dancers. As many as two hundred performers, grouped in highly formalized patterns, participated in other magnificent royal entertainments. Some of them, dating from Silla dynasty King Hŏn'gang's reign (876-886), such as *Ch'ŏyong* Dance or "The Dance of the Dragon of the Eastern Sea", indicate the cross-cultural exchanges of music and dance with T'ang China.

Korean art was highly prized at the T'ang court: three Koguryŏ dances were included in the classic repertory, and two of them were immortalized by poets. Yi Po wrote:[5]

> Crowned in a golden hat the dancer
> Like a white colt turns slowly,
> The white sleeves fluttering against the wind
> Like a bird from the Eastern Sea.

When it was performed in China, Yi Po's lines were sung with the dance.

Far more than being just the passive go-between or cultural transmitter of Chinese arts to Japan, it must be recognized that Korean artists created many of the best music and dance forms given to both countries. Japan's artistic debt to Korea is enormous. As early as 285 A.D. Korean artists introduced what became the beginning of Japanese music. In 548 more musicians were sent to Japan. During the Paekche dynasty, the Korean Mimaji, returning from the T'ang court, introduced China's masked comedy pantomime to Japan in 612 A.D. Known as *gigaku*, it was popularly sustained at the court in Nara.

Gigaku featured the lion dance and a low-comedy triangle scene over the *Lady of Go* — the only woman character — culminating in a fight between a strong man and her servant, who succeeded in twisting off the penis of the aggressor. It concluded with a Bacchic revel for a Persian king and his retinue, each wearing a mask expressing a different condition of drunkenness. Two hundred and fifty superb wooden masks are still preserved in Nara, the ancient capital of Japan; the word Nara itself is Korean.

But *gigaku* faded in popularity with the later introduction of *gagaku* and *bugaku*, more sophisticated expressions again received from China through Korea. *Gagaku* (Celestial Music) and *bugaku* the dance which goes with it, are that great collection of court music and dances which the T'ang emperors acquired from thirteen adjacent territories. Though these have long since disappeared from their original East Indian and Vietnamese origins, the Imperial Household Music Department of Japan has preserved and continues to maintain this unmatched treasury of Asian forms. The repertory is divided into alternating groups: the Left (costumed in red) from China and the Right (costumed in green) from Korea.

The *Ch'ŏyong* or Dragon of The Eastern Sea—Dance is a remarkable Korean classic. Originally a solo, later a duet, and by the early Yi dynasty, a quintet, performed as an exorcism of all evils at the court before the New Year, the men, each wearing a brown faced mask and having individual costumes of blue, white, red, black and yellow (signifying the five directions or four cardinal points and center) perform solo turning sequences, then each dances in duet with the center figure, and all turn in unison. The music is a shaman song; the masks may have a link to Tibet; the use of long white sleeves may derive from China.

Titles of the Korean court dances project images of birds and flowers: "Beautiful Persons Picking Peonies," "The Coming of the Phoenix," "The Nightingale" and "The Crane Dance." The Sword Dance, performed today only by women, is a weapons dance which makes no pretense to swordsmanship, being a playfully percussive spectacle. These genteel subjects reflect sophisticated delicacy of taste, with quiet humor, as in the "Ballgame Dance," where two teams of women compete throwing wooden balls through the holes in two flower-bedecked gates. Those who succeed in making the goal receive a peony flower, those who fail receive a black line painted on one cheek by a 'brush girl.' The tossing, awarding of prizes and penalties are all executed in flowing rhythmic movement, the whole preceded by ushers with standards, who sing opening and closing songs.

The classical "Nightingale Dance" requires greatest control for it is performed in the least space and is slowest of all. The main interest is the succession of accents with the rainbow-banded long flowing sleeves. The *Jiuta Mai* of classical Japanese dance is also limited to a single mat-size space, and the dancer must sustain her motions with her *furosode* (very long sleeves). But where the *Jiuta Mai* is consistently suppressed emotion, in slow motion, the nightingale dance has several changes of tempo, and the whole spirit is one of lightness and joy, with only a suggestion of a smile on the composed features.

King Sejong, the great Yi dynasty monarch who ascended the throne in 1397 "gave himself over to music and dance as much as he did to literature, astronomy and the fine arts." He classified music and dance into three sections and adjusted the costumes of the court musicians and dancers. His grandson King Sŏngjong sponsored the writing of the great comprehensive book on Korean music and dance, the *Akhak Kwoebŏm* (Standard of Musical Science), which describes the dances, costumes, properties, procedures and instruments used to this day in recreating these ancient works of art.

Korea is fortunate to have these priceless glories from the past and today's artists who can reconstruct them at the National Classical Institute of Music. The earliest records show that the noble court youths, the *hwarang* (flower boys of Silla), preceded the women court dancers. At one time the masculine corps danced only for the king and his ministers; women dancers appeared only before the queen and her court. After the fall of Silla, the *hwarang* were and became either full-fledged shamans, or strolling players, and then the *kisaeng* became the royal entertainers, as well as the best and only educated women in Korea, similar to the equivalent Japanese *geisha* (arts person).

The court *Hang-mu* (Crane Dance) has two lotus buds on a rear platform and two dancers costumed as enormous cranes. As the dance evolves, the giant birds peck at the lotus buds with their long bills, the petals unfold and child dancers appear. A similar piece has the same emergent-from-lotus-bud children, and two large storks as bird-principals. Peonies and lotus flowers are, of course, Buddhist-derived symbols.

The performers of the court dance repertory today, trained and visible at the National Classical Music and Dance Institute, present exquisite appearance in magnificent costumes with small flower crowns of gold, glistening with pendants. The necklines are high, the voluminous skirts are gathered over flattened breasts, the hands are concealed in rainbow-banded long sleeves which trail on the ground, their stockinged legs and unique Korean turned-up-toed-slippers (rarely seen unless the skirts swing away from their ankles in occasional turns) — these are de-personalized sex-diminished images, more like flowers than humans. One marvels at the control, the splendid carriage of the body, the quiet grace and always that lilting pulse from the chest into the shoulders with the arms outstretched which suggest birds winging through the air without effort, an art which conceals art.

Buddhist Dances

Buddhism, the most permissive of religions, came to Korea from India, via China in 372 A.D. The monk Chin Kam, who learned Buddhist chanting known as *Pŏmp'ae* in T'ang China, returned to Korea in 830 (Silla dynasty), bringing that music and four dances associated it. These dances can be observed at certain ceremonies in the temples of married monks. Designed to "supplicate Lord Buddha so that the souls of the departed may be permitted entrance to Nirvana," the first three together are known as *Chak-pŏb* (Making the Law).

Serenely beautiful is the *Nabi-ch'um* (Butterfly Dance), and this one is also performed by Buddhist nuns; the *Para-ch'um* (Cymbal Dance) performed by two or four monks, requires strength and agility, for the large heavy brass cymbals must be swung rhythmically up and behind the head. The *Pŏbkko-ch'um* (Law Drum Dance) solo involves playing the large temple drum played with two sticks. Since 1950 the secular version exploits almost acrobatic movement: the body wings in half-circles at first then in full circles of the upper body from a complete back-bend position, at the same time the dancer builds up ecstaticly frenzied rhythmic development while beating the drum.

On a Royal Asiatic Society outing, we came across a memorial funeral service held outdoors in a field in front of a temple, brilliantly decorated with banners of the five colors, and huge paintings of Buddhist saints strung up back of an altar richly laden with flowers, fruits, colored rice cakes, candles and incense. Three monks led the mourners in procession around the space, beating drums, cymbals, and playing the trumpet. A pair of monks performed the impressive cymbal dance, swinging them to and fro, twisting their bodies in spiral turns, deftly revolving them rapidly in spirals, sometimes holding them upside down, softly clashing one on top of the other. Generally the vibrations — sonorous and booming — were strong enough to exorcize any evil spirit.

Then the oldest monk donned the special white dancing robe with very wide and deep long trailing sleeves, and the embroidered peaked hat, both of which suggest the form of a butterfly. Over one shoulder he wore the red *kasa*, the monk's cloth bag (originally designed to receive food when begging, now a decorative graded badge of office). With a pink peony in his left and a white peony in his right hand, he bowed to the altar and temple; slowly, reverently opening his arms, and leaning backward, he looked down — a movement similar to the worship gesture of Shinto shrine dancers in Japan. With deep knee bends, and small shoulder circles, he moved his arms and shoulders softly up and down, in and out, and crossed one flower over the other three times in low level. The slow sustained revolution evoked benedictions of grace and proclaimed at the same time the joyous Buddhist philosophy toward death, celebrating the transformation of the soul epitomized by the metamorphosis of a butterfly. Unlike the cymbal dance, this breathed peacefulness. The other two monks repeated the cymbal dance afterward, the two together, the Yin and Yang of their belief.

On the great festival of Buddha's Birthday when the temples become at evening a glowing maze of lighted lanterns, lotus or peony shaped, and the faithful address the huge paintings of the Saints hung up behind the main altar, rising and falling to their knees like the waves of the sea, we can observe the monks at Pongwŏn-sa Temple (behind Ewha Womans University) making law visible with true masculine strength and dignity in these dances.

The fourth Buddhist dance — the *Pŏbkkoch'um* (Law Drum Dance) is an intensely thrilling solo for a dancer using two sticks, but the drum is considerably smaller than the largest Buddhist drum. It begins with a dramatic rolling of the sticks around the ridges of the drum's circumference, invoking the spirit and gradually builds to a crescendo of passionate drumming.

It is this dance, popularized, completely separated from the temple and religious connotation, which is now performed with five, nine, or as many as twelve dancers and so many small drums, each within a stand, making a grand batterie *tour de force* of rhythmic dexterity combined with acrobatic movement to sensational effect. Buddhism has thus contributed an enormously effective dance to the professional art stage. Performed by glamorously made-up smiling young ladies it is now secular, decorative, and usually the stimulating high point of most dance performances. A dramatic legend is sometimes applied to this dance, called *sŭng-mu* (Monk's Dance). A sixteenth century *kisaeng,* renowned as poet, musician, dancer and irresistable paramour, was determined to seduce a particular monk of irreproachable celibacy. She visited his temple, donned Buddhist robes and hat and performed the thrilling drum patterns with the two sticks, at the end, disrobing completely, when the poor monk, overwhelmed, capitulated. In the hands of a skilfull dancer the tension between the erotic power of the dancer and the conflict with the drum symbolizing Buddhist law, can become a real experience.

Folk Dance

While kings, princes, knights, professionals have all danced at court, and the monks in temples, historically one of the oldest forms of all is the strenuous outdoor farmers dance — an expression of the folk. This has astonishing vigor and rhythmic verve. Leading a procession of men and boys, a bearer carries a pole with pheasant feathers at the top (the ghost or spirit symbol) and a banner proclaiming: "Agriculture is the foundation of the universe." The dancers' hats are decorated with huge pompoms of white paper flowers of Buddhist influence. They accompany themselves with hand-held drums, gongs, a piercingly loud reed instrument, and several *changgo* (double-barrelled drums) beaten with two kinds of bamboo sticks. Following the leader's running, hopping, turning, they move counterclockwise and the exuberance never dies. Each one in turn dances solo with his particular instrument, they circle in union and it comes to a climax when smaller boys take center and rotate their heads producing long eccentric spirals with the white ribbons attached to the special swivel in the crown of their hats. They gyrate standing up and lying down and the flowing streamers' parabolas in the air make a joyous ending.

The farmers dance — typically virile — is performed by both men and women today, but the circular *Kanggang-suwŏlle* is purely feminine, performed on the full moon of the first and eighth lunar calendar month, by a large group of girls to their own singing of solo verse and chorus. It starts very slowly, moving clock, then counterclockwise and accelerates to a rapid whirling ecstatic climax. One feels as long as these folk traditions continue to flourish, Korea will never become decadent.

Since 1961, the government sponsors the National Folk Arts Contest, awarding prizes to the best dance groups, held each year in a different city. Such not-to-be-missed occasions include all the traditional expressions of the people, except the classical court dance. So when we see the girl's dedicatory opening "Fan Dance" we are actually seeing a popularization of the shaman's solo dance, with costumes derived from T'ang court dress, and the fan elaborated with large floral-designs, the groupings themselves suggesting opening, closing, or turning flowers. The shaman dance is so popular it dominates the 'classical' in the sense of traditional, folk expression.

Though the farmers dance may have Buddhist-type hats, it is even more a shaman-connected rite. In the villages, the bands of players go from house to house, performing a shaman *kut*, with their exuberant rhythms and ear-splitting noise, enough to drive away all the evil spirits and invoke all the good.

By the term folk dance, then, we must liberally understand it to mean any dance which represents the tradition of the Korean people, exclusive of the court. And the intermingling of Buddhist with shaman forms, and shaman rites with Buddhist rites, with some slight tinge of Confucianism over all, is to be expected as normal, since Korea is rich in all three ancient traditions. The present government encouragement given to these native forms is a healthy manifestation of Korea's spirit expressed in the Intangible Arts. But when we see what looks like American Musical Comedy style creeping into the large group dances, we can only hope that native choreographers will cherish and keep what is unique to Korea in its purity, and not let the dances disappear in a false vogue for Hollywoodian westernization.

Mask Dance Drama

In ancient days ritual-dance-drama was one inseparable entity relating man to the powers greater than himself. Masks were sacred, essential and needed for many purposes both magical and practical, and later artistic. Dr. Yi Tu-hyŏn tells us a third century Yi tribe performed a religious service to tigers (who are gods of mountains), and the *Ho-mu* (Tiger Dance) was performed till late in the Yi dynasty. Among the ten different mask dances surviving today, one is that remnant from *gigaku*, the lion dance, performed by two dancers under one cloth. Originally the lion — an avatar of Buddha — appeared as a threat to eat the bad characters; but now even the depraved monks entertain him by dancing, so he is satisfied. The Korean lion is singularly relaxed, with shaggy coat, sometimes on extra pair of goggle eyes wobbling on a spring. A monkey is included to imitate the other characters.

In the Koryŏ period (935-1133) the beginnings of verse-drama, originally performed by a single dancer, developed into grand dancing dramas for end-of-the-year ceremonies. Gradually, Dr. Yi says five plays were integrated into a whole.[9] These pastoral-comical-satirical farces with very ancient roots, open and close with rituals to the gods. In between we are treated to episodes with masked shamans, monks, farmers, wives, *kisaeng*, concubines, *yangbans* and servants — the whole spectrum of feudal society's inevitable conflict between ages, sexes and classes dramatized, with pantomime, comic dialogue, intermittent singing and dancing, together with the extraordinary stylization of the masks, which create a strong impression.

In one scene a midwife helps produce a baby (doll); the mother abandons it; the father gives it a cautionary sermon. Corrupt lecherous monks, not very bright *yangbans*, quarreling husbands-wives-concubines receive the most humorous commentary.

At first the rhythms are heavy in slow six beats, which change to faster twelve-beat patterns, with the same primitive vigor and strength of the farmers' dance. From deep knee bounds, (also like the farmers' dance) there is much flinging of one leg upward, making the long sleeves fly in the air. The male characters vibrate their bodies from the hips upward, shake their shoulders, protrude their heads, step and leap or hop with enormous gusto. The characteristic movement is to jump into second position (feet apart), knees deeply bent, while lifting the shoulders on one, slowly shift the body to the side and make a syncopated head thrust sharply on three *And*.

Uniquely important in themselves, the Korean masks represent a link in the development of the ultimate Japanese masks of Noh. Two of them relate to the earlier magnificent masks of *gigaku*: the *Hahoe* man's mask with moveable jaw, and the *Kaksi* the strongly modeled woman's face with braided hair looped on one side. *Gigaku* masks, made of paulownia wood, cover the entire head; the Korean masks made of wood, or gourds, sometimes paper and fur, cover the face only and the players first don a black cloth to conceal the back and sides of the head and neck.

As in the ancient *Ch'ŏyong* dance, the colors of the costumes symbolize the five directions: blue-East, red-South, white-West, black-North and yellow-Center. Thus when the black-masked old monk is defeated by the youthful prodigal red-faced *Ch'wibari*, or the black-faced old first wife is defeated by the young white-faced concubine, we have the symbolic victory of Summer over Winter.[10] Comically appealing is the young girl's Picasso-ésque lopsided nose and simpering smile on one side of her face; the old nobleman's small white-fur-tufted eyebrows and whiskers; repellant, the old woman's black face with red-and-white polka dots, the bumps and ridges on the "Boil Monk's" face, suitable for a renegade from holy vows, the sly villain in seduction scenes.

The best place to see the mask dance drama is in the country, where the actors first file through the village streets, pausing at every house for blessing, then proceed along a rice-paddy ridge onto the open hillside against the mountain background, making a primordial dramatic procession with the masks worn on top of their heads, like figures out of a European fairy-tale. The mask dance drama group from Yuyang-ni, Yangju County, which has been named a Korean National Treasure, keep a strong tradition. They perform on Buddha's Birthday, at *Ch'usŏk* and other festival times. The players, most of them men, have been doing this for years, and their style has authority and ease.

A good performance depends upon the improvisational ability of the players who banter each other in dialogue, arouse the audience to answer questions asked, to shout comments, clap their hands rhythmically and sometimes join in the satirical refrains of the songs. The general revel which concludes the performance, with most of the audience, especially youthful ones, immediately pouring out onto the space, everyone dancing in robust dance-drama style to the shrilling trumpet, makes a truly affirmative life-enhancing ending. The Yangju masks are burned in a final ritual, one more proof that this expression goes deeper than casual amusement. The masks are sacred and must be recreated for each performance. To watch this celebration in the spring-green countryside with a peaceful cow dominating the horizon for contrast, is to feel the Lesser Dionysian spirit, and with the ritualized dedication to the gods, a sanctification of the comic urge.

Shaman Dance

As mentioned before, Confucianism did nothing for the lower classes except to keep them in their place and Buddhism originally was for the upper classes. But Shamanism — "the archaic technique of ecstasy" in Eliade's phrase — from earliest times served the people's need for the divine spirit. The shaman (Tungusic word) is literally the medium who brings the spirit or the ghost from Heaven to man; figuratively, a priest, a conjuror; loosely a medicine man, a tribal worker of magic, a magic healer. It is the primitive religion of Northern Ural-Altaic Asia, Northern Europe and some North and South American Indians, wherever gods, ancestral spirits, ghosts or demons respond to the shamans as mediumistic magicians. The Chinese character for the word shaman symbolizes this clearly, written with two straight horizontal lines signifying Heaven and Earth, the vertical line between the two, representing the shaman, the bridge between, and the two triangles on either side of the line representing man.[11]

Of the two types of shamans — those who become so through heredity, or those who acquire it by visitation of the spirit, (the *Kangsin-mu* [drops from Heaven] which then has to be authenticated by an older shaman, with special initiation rites) — the inheritance type prevails in southern Korea; the acquired type is found in northern Korea. Of all the Asiatic varieties, Korean Shamanism is the most highly developed and complex in form. A proper in-depth evaluation of Shamanism needs the combined disciplines of anthropology, art, history, sociology, aesthetics, psychiatry and religion, plus several life-times in which to observe and then correlate all the findings. Since I have only a dancer's discipline, I will try to limit my focus to the shaman's efficacy as expressed in dance, if necessarily stepping into the fields of myth, ritual, religion and therapy along the way.

In Korea, the word *mudang* (*Mu*, shaman; *dang*, house) applies to either male or female mediums; the male priests are

Dancing shaman with swords

As healer and artist-entertainer

also called *paksu*. The *mudang* is supremely at home in the realm of ecstatic possession of the spirit — her ancestors, or her guardians. She is prophetess, diviner, healer, psychopomp and artist-entertainer.

> I have to dance and sing. (Goes a shaman song.)
> My heart is quiet when the wind blows
> From the big mountain.
> My heart endures strong as the bamboo or pine tree
> Against evil spirits.
> All joyful, really joyous, I have to dance and sing.

In Suzanne Langer's philosophy, the purpose of all the arts is to create illusions: music, for example, creates the illusion of time: painting the illusion of space; drama, the illusion of history; and dance she says creates the illusion of virtual powers.[13] The shaman's business is to create illusions too; her powers are not only physical but also magical, psychic and spiritual.

Shaman rites contain primitive, in the sense of primary, original, elements. In addition to altar services with fruits, flowers, incense, candles and many kinds of rice-cakes and rice grain, a pig's head, pig's feet, sometimes a cow or ox-head, and chicken are offerings. But from the formal point of view the ceremonies are not primitive at all; they are highly organized and complex. And the shaman's singing, dancing, divining, healing exorcisms are designed to bring happiness, longevity, prosperity to her people. She may pray for her own household but she does not pray just for herself, she prays from concern for others.

From birth to death there are many occasions for the shaman's services. At birth, a mother presents the shaman with the child's name and birth date on a piece of cloth; the *mudang* becomes its spirit- or god-mother, the child her spiritual ward. The *mudang* must be consulted about the vicissitudes, the uncertainties of health and fortune, about house removals or troubled human relationships. And only a *mudang* has the power to ask a sick spirit to leave. At death, the shaman conducts the souls' passage to the underworld. The ceremonies have fixed dates or may be performed on demand.[14]

The ancient hold of Shamanism on the people is understandable. In Korea's cosmological myth, the first human being was created when the virgin goddess *aegissi*, in Heaven, married a divine priest and gave birth to three brothers, (who became the birth gods), producing men on earth. These gods

Mudang as supreme prophetess   Worshippers of Shamanism

predestine children and are responsible for bringing them up. A man's honor, wealth, fortune depend upon the gods; death is given by the gods of the underworld. When a man dies their messenger leads him with a rope around his neck to Hades, where for seven days and nights he must journey to the ten different palaces of the gods ruling there, to be judged by each in turn for the good or evil deeds committed while on earth. Good men go to Paradise and eternal life; bad ones remain to suffer in Hell. A discontented soul, also the ghosts of the unmarried, or of suicides or of murdered persons can return and may cause sickness or trouble on earth. Not only men but all things are governed by the gods. And the shaman is the controlling link to their power.

Some of Korea's earliest kings had shamanist names. The magnificent royal crowns with symmetrical deer antlers rising high, festooned with amulets, and all of gold, to be seen in the National Museum of Art today, are said to relate to the ancient Turkish shaman cult of the deer.

The consensus is that Shamanism is the oldest, the basic religion of the Korean people. The imported religions of Confucianism and Buddhism overlay it but did not change its fundamental structure. Certainly the latter religions helped to enrich its form. The ten kings (Buddhist Saints), the image of Buddha himself, attended by the Sun and Moon deities, the Mountain Spirit, the Dragon God, two Chinese Generals, scholars and acolytes often depicted on the walls of shaman altars, are of mixed Buddhist-Taoist influence. Alan Heyman writes that thirty percent of the twelve part *kut* (ceremony) is Buddhistic.[15] The lotus symbolism, the use of brass cymbals, the bell, the Buddhist monk's costume, the head-to-floor bowing with arms extended, palms facing up, used by the shaman bespeak Buddha worship.

Confucianism, at its height in the Yi dynasty, repudiated Shamanism, officially suppressing it; they had to turn in their books, which were burned and the shamans were banished from the capital. Nevertheless, the hapless Queen Min (who was murdered by the Japanese in 1895) elevated her favorite sorceress to the rank of princess, gave her the name of Yi Chiyong, brought her and Shamanism into the palace, and erected Kuksadang, a national spirit shrine, on Mt. Inwang which is in occasional use in Seoul, today. Near the top of beautiful walled Inwang mountain and within half-hour walking distance, to the north of Fulbright House, the signboard near the Kuksadang shrine states:

> The enshrined house of T'aejo, first Yi dynasty king, Sung Yi and his great commanders of self preservation. Built in the reign of the second king and named Kuksadang. Here King and Queen T'aejo enshrined the gods of heaven, mountain, sea, Muhak Kuksa (advisor to T'aejo).
>
> General Ch'oe Yŏng and the great commanders of East, West and South gather here to pray for the national peace and prosperity. The paintings of the gods were painted in 1623. Now many witches and wizards gather here and perform religious service for the nation's peace and prosperity and often perform exorcism for the individual.

Like the Turkish *qut* (happiness); the Mongolian *qutug*; and the Tungusic *kutu*, the Korean word *kut* (shamanistic séance) implies the creation of happiness in positive terms. Sometimes *kut* is called '*p'uri*' (to untie or solve). It indicates a mythic "world in which gods and man have direct dialogue; the sacred and profane co-exist....the mythical world before sacred deities and profane man were divided, before Yin and Yang were separated. The male shaman dances in female costume, the *mudang* dances in military helmet and man's official coat. The *kut* is the regeneration of the aboriginal world of oneness...(man) merging with the god himself."[16]

"We thank the Heavens, the Mountain Spirit, the Ancestor Spirit, the Earth Spirit," writes Ŭiji San, contemporary shaman living in Seoul. Shaman worship generally is for the spirits of Heaven, the Sun, the Moon, the Seven Stars, the Mountain God — (the beneficent white-haired old man sitting under a pine tree with a tiger curled around his feet, as the wonderful folk-art paintings love to depict him) —, Earth, Water and Road Spirits; Fire, Wind, Tree and Stone Spirits; at the gods of agriculture, of birth and disease, and the ten gods of Hell; kings, queens, princesses, commanding generals and their wives, and Buddhist and Taoist saints make up the pantheon.

The pattern of séances begins with invoking the spirit, receiving an oracle from the spirit, and returning the spirit to the other world. A full shaman ceremony may have as many as twelve or up to twenty-four *kŏri*, or services.

For dancing, the *mudang* uses long sleeves, scarves, fans, wands, bells; knives of several lengths, swords, tridents and scimitars. Sometimes she dances with a whole pig strapped to her back, or with a cow head balanced and tied upon her head. Spectacular use is made of a long white banner, which assistants hold horizontally about waist level high, and as the *mudang* runs through it, it rips apart, symbolizing the final stage of her spiritual journey in Hell on behalf of the ghost. A similar "spirit path" — a long strip of white cloth may lead from the altar inside her home to the outdoor high platform on which she dances on knives.

For divination purposes she uses rice, coins, chopsticks, bells, shaking a tree, sometimes a turtle. To demonstrate her magical powers she makes the trident and scimitar stand alone. Her supreme accomplishment is to receive the spirit and then dance standing barefoot on the edges of blades (used for cutting straw), standing high above the ground, which is a real feat of balance. Unsupported, she leans backward, bows and prays to the cardinal directions, and divines from a lofty level.

As actress she cajoles, teases, scolds, encourages, comforts, weeps for and prays over her clients; she supplicates then obeys the wishes of her guardian spirits. And always when dancing she concentrates on the spirit. A *mudang* who recently became too interested in the dance more as a dancer than as *mudang*, was criticized by her peers in thus failing to concentrate on the spirit world which is her true domain.[17]

A fascinating problem in considering shaman dance is to distinguish between the progressive states of ecstasy-trance-possession and the movement patterns involved. Not all ecstasy goes into trance; not all trance into possession. But the shaman's function as medium between man and the spirit world requires an altered state of consciousness, easily achieved in the simple act of rhythmic motion of the dance, stimulated by repetitive vibrations from drum and clashing cymbals. Rhythmical motion is itself euphoric and therapeutic. As Curt Sachs says: "Dance is and gives ecstasy."[18] Infused with spirit, the material body transcends itself and becomes light.

The word ecstasy [Greek *ex* (out of) — *stasis* (order, balance)] was once equated with swoon or trance, now obsolete. Four livelier definitions are: the state of being beside oneself; beyond reason and self control; (second) the state of overmastering feeling, especially of joy, rapture or delight; (third) violent distraction, madness; and (fourth) in mystical language, the psychological state of intense absorption in divine things accompanied by loss of sense perception and depression of the vital functions.

Let us rush to the defense of the shaman at once by insisting, with Miccea Eliade, that unlike the psychotic personality, the shaman is always in control of her behavior.[19] At some moments she may be inspired to improvise, but most of her actions are traditional, ordered and measured, not incoherent but repeated at will. Functioning as priestess, dancer, actress (comedienne and tragedienne) diviner, healer, psychopomp, with changes of costume and properties for as many as twenty-four different *kŏri* in a continuous marathon of several days and nights, she sustains what no one 'beyond reason or self-control' could possibly perform. Perhaps she may reach a moment or two of madness — as don't we all? — or seem to swoon, but these are fleeting states in her functioning of the divine will. As performer, she is prodigious.

Korean dance in general manifests a supremely ecstatic quality. The paradigm of the soul or spirit of Korea is the shaman's ecstatic dance.

The condition of trance of course implies a more negative state than ecstasy. The word itself from old French *transir* (to pass, usually from life; Latin *transire* (to pass over), receives five distinctions from the dictionary: (first) "to pass from life, to die, to lose consciousness, to swoon; (second) to be in great suspense or benumbed by fear; (third) the state of suspense or uncertainty, partly suspended animation or of ability to function; a daze, a stupor; and (fourth) a sleepless state such as that of deep hypnosis, appearing in hysteria and spiritualistic mediums with limited sensory contact and subsequent amnesia of what occurred during that state." Fifth (actually listed first) trance is — (not so helpfully for our purpose) — equated with ecstasy, rapture that destroys one's consciousness of surroundings.

We all know the state of 'mindless trance' exhibited by adolescents in our current youth culture, in the collective "Rock" expression. Drugged and deafened by electronically amplified sounds, they move with eyes partly or fully closed, repeating a few gestures over and over, not wanting to see or be part of the real world from which they are escaping. Unconscious of their surroundings, unaware of their detached partners, the self surrenders to the most primitive level. Rock dancers are truly in trance, out of this world. From the dance point of view this, with minimum form, is purely instinctive or reflexive animal behavior.

In extreme forms, then, trance can go into stupor; ecstasy into madness. Saint Bhodi Dharma who remained in the same static position for nine years exemplifies the former; the ancient Greek Maenads, at the opposite pole, passed from ecstasy into the state of Bacchic possession and in their wine-and-poppy-induced 'enthousiasmos' (full of the god), insanely tore living animals to pieces.

Possession is the state of being possessed or dominated by an extraneous personality, a daemon, a passion, idea or impulse, according to Webster. The Spanish Flamenco gypsy dancer waits for the *duende* (imp, spirit, or ghost), which mysteriously comes from the ground into his feet, before he can dance a step. No *duende*, no dance. Different from trance or ecstasy, possession by the spirit can lead to extraordinary behavior. Southeast Asia offers many types of trance-possession dances, three of which I have seen for comparison.

In Bali, the "Trance Dance of the Virgins," performed by so-called Reverend Angels, two small girls about ten years old — the children are already in trance when they first appear borne on the shoulders of two men, coming through the split-tower gate of the temple. One lighted incense stick glows in each of their flower-crowns. Their eyes are half-closed when they are put down on the matting and begin to dance in the dreamy Legong manner to a melody sung by a women's chorus. At the end of the song, the leader claps her hands as a signal to the men's chorus opposite, who break into the rapid staccato rhythm of the monkey chant, "Chak-chak-chak-chak." This sends the girls whirling clockwise rapidly, til unwinding counterclockwise, they fall senseless to the ground, the sign that the protective goddesses of the village have entered their bodies. Women attendants stroke their foreheads, smoothe their hair, and set them up on their still-tranced feet again to repeat this alternation of elegant dance with ecstatic whirling, losing consciousness, as many as seven or eight times in one session. Finally, their crowns removed, the priest sprinkles them with holy water. Restored to themselves, they are shepherded away.

This exorcism for some sickness or evil is followed by a trance-possession dance for a man, a fire-walker, in the same village, and for the same purpose. Here we can see the priest's preparation, who smokes, then blows the smoke into the face of the dancer before he performs. The firewalker has a hobbyhorse costume made of fringed palm leaves which conceal most of his body and arch over his head in a combination suggestion of horseman, tail, and partial mask. He squats before the priest, inhaling the smoke. Shortly after, his head falls to one side. Suddenly he whirls around, crouched on the ground, leaps up and trots, then gallops several times around the outer circle of the center bonfire of palm branches, which have been set ablaze sometime before. Finally he prances through the hot flames and coals scattering them with his feet. Approaching the fire from different directions, he does this over and over again, until the fire is burnt out. It takes two men a considerable time to quiet his galvanic movements. Even after his arms and legs cease to thrash, the horse-hand between his legs continues to buck and tremble. Again as at the beginning the priest comes with holy water, and gives him something to drink. Gradually the seated dancer opens his eyes. Though he had been in and out of the flames a dozen times, there was no sign of burning on his body or the soles of his feet.

In *Sokkari*, a Sri Lankan folk play, the young boy playing the king-hero's role, is required to become possessed by the spirit of the goddess Pantini (Singhalese version of Parvati). Occasionally sips of wine may help; but the ritual worship of Pantini, the actual gesture of adoration itself, expressed in monotonous repetition of a few steps and hops forward and backward while holding high in both hands a large red palm flower, and thrusting the flower toward the shrine with a deep therapic impulse from the chest, is physiologically enough to induce hyper-oxygenization. The repetition of this galvanic offering continues until suddenly the flower darts upward into the sky and the king-hero, unconscious, pitches forward.

The guru-leader of the players closely follows and antici-pates the moment of possession. He directs the 'assistants,' to catch the actor as he falls and hold him in horizontal position until his thrashing arms and legs relax. Restored to his feet, the boy rests for a while in a chair, then resumes his acting-dancing-singing role for several more hours, if with much less vitality than before.

In both Bali and Sri Lanka, inherited predisposition for trance occurs. A contagious phenomenon, it can affect the audience too, which can be dangerous if there are not enough priests to control, and help to bring them all out of their trances successfully. Both the Singhalese and Balinese god-possession dances differ from real shaman ones, because the possessed do not travel to the other world, as real shamans do. Instead they "invite the god or spirit into their own bodies, within reach of the community, and for their benefit." [20]

Our final comparison will be with Korea's neighbor, Japan. As in Korea, Shamanism is considered to be the oldest indigenous religion there too, from earliest times. The first Japanese dance is attributed to the heavenly nymph Uzume, who turned a tub upside down and sang and danced ecstatically upon it, until her skirt string was loosened — (or, some versions have it) — she pushed her skirts, below her hips. Whereupon the eighty myriad gods and goddesses of the high heavens filled the sky with their laughter. This piqued the curiosity of Amaterasu, Great Sky Shiner, the Sun-Goddess who was hiding in a cave, so that she peeked out to see what was going on. She was drawn from the cave, which was then barred with twisted rope — a taboo sign — so that she could never go back. Thus light returned to the world, and the eighty myriad deities joined hands and danced and sang because, after having been plunged in darkness, the world never looked so fair. Uzume's properties included bunches of bamboo grass and bells on a stick, similar to shaman bells in Korea. Because of that original up-turned tub, all stages in Japan are considered sacred to this day, and all Japanese performers claim divine descent from Uzume, the primal goddess of dance, magic and music. Many elements of Uzume's possession-dance, in this delightful legend, are typical shamanist behavior.

The earliest Chinese records of Japan, mention a few empresses renowned for their ability as sorceresses. Sorcery and divination were part of the duties of the vestal virgin attendants — the *Miko* — of Shinto shrines, a practice which in some places continues today. The *Miko* serve the *kami* with prayer dances of thanksgiving, or for health, fortune, good harvests, and sons. Anyone who makes the appropriate contribution at the admission gate may have the service of a *kagura* (the music and dance performed in the presence of the god) performed at larger Shinto shrines today. The *kagura* dancers have white-painted faces and rouged underlips. They wear wide-sleeved, long-trained transparent white robes over red dancing skirts, and have plastic flowers in their hair. They move slowly with quiet grace, breathing serenity and harmony with nature to simple beating of clappers, the sounds of a flute, or a chant. The movement style has undoubtedly been influenced by the elegant restraint of Bugaku Court dance from T'ang China. But some of the primitive rapturous ecstatic quality is still to be seen in the Shinto *tsurugi* (sword) *kagura*, where a dancer, or pair of *Miko*, each with short swords in hands, dip, dive, and run in the four directions, and clash the naked steel blades against each other in quick in-and-out successions. In between whirling, they stand with closed eyes and talk to the *kami*. This quickness of movement and intention is similar to Korean shaman exorcistic trance dance with the swords.

The ultimate Japanese example is the classic art of the *Noh* theater, which sums up a thousand years of myth, legend, ritual and history, as it was crystallized in the fourteenth century, and is performed today largely unchanged, except that, surprisingly enough, the tempo has actually become slower than it was originally. A superb, often breathtaking balance of poetry, music and mask dance — considered by many to be Japan's supreme aesthetic accomplishment — the ghost plays of *Noh* are essentially shaman rituals. The plays are introduced by the *Waki* ('stands aside') character, usually a Buddhist priest, who, on a journey, introduces the scene, becomes aware of some emanation there, and as medium, invokes the spirit of the place. Then the *Shite* (principal character) who alone wears the mask and dances, as if arriving from another world, appears at the far end of the bridge stage. He may be guised as a divinity, as elemental or supernatural being, a warrior-ghost, the shade of a jealous woman or some other tormented human character. Arriving at the main stage, he signs of and dances out his fate. The *Waki* exorcizes the troubles of the soul wandering in Hell, by rubbing his beads and saying his Buddhist prayers, at the end sending it back to the spirit world on its journey to perfection or Nirvana. Miraculously these shaman rites have metamorphosed themselves into the world's most sophisticated theatre of abstract forms. No wonder *Noh* plays are hypnotic; they are Shamanism glorified to aesthetic perfection.

Having observed (if only superficially) trance possession dance in Bali, Sri Lanka and Japan, we find Korean expression to be elaborately developed and carried to an extraordinary Dionysian level.

Shaman Movements

In Seoul city, and Yuyang-ni village, Yangju County, the dancing takes place next to the altars in the shaman's homes, sometimes overflowing into adjacent rooms, or even outdoors in the courtyard, but in a necessarily restricted space. At Kuksadang, the free area for movement seemed to be a mere ten by two feet; perhaps four by five in the village house and at comparatively wealthy grandmother Chŏn's possibly eight by four feet. The small scale of the space reflects the humble position of the shamans today. Once highest of all and divinely respected in the ancient religion, they have dropped to the bottom of the social ladder, along with peddlers and the outcasts who butcher meat or work with leather, fur or feathered creatures. "King of the Despised," legendary Princess Pari called herself, a title descriptive of their own status and so adopted by all shamans. Parenthetically, Princess Pari, the seventh daughter of a royal couple, was cruelly mistreated by her parents. Her spirit, wandering in Hell, came across a potent flower which she carried back to earth and with it brought her dead parents back to life. Endowed with the gift of guiding souls to the other world, Princess Pari became deified and is now one of the chief shaman deities.

As dance movement is necessarily limited by space, the principal directions the shamans freely move in is up, or around, in one spot. The characteristic action — appropriate for the spirit world — is jumping. The shamans in fact describe what they are doing as "jumping." With boundless vitality an old *mudang* may spring eighty times in one spot; a young person dancing in the general celebration at grandmother Chŏn's jumped over a thousand times. When they have received the spirit, they tirelessly spring into the air ecstatically swinging their long-sleeved arms up and down, in and out, or in wave motion.

The other typical motion is turning — that instinctive action which healthy children express and grown-ups may remember as blissful sensation, whirling oneself around until the whole world seems to spin, and one falls limp and helpless to the ground. Usually they hold their arms out in side extension, using wands, scarves, fans, or bells in their hands. When turning with knives, or swords, the points are held variously at hip level, or the back of the shoulders, sometimes crossed low in front, or at head level. They turn, as the Dervish do in their communion with God, in the continuous round which is the symbol of perfection and harmony. The most spectacular of turns is when they rotate with a whole pig strapped across their back, or with a cow — or ox-head on top of the head.

Transitional movements working up to the state of trance-possession are walking back and forth in ellipses, rising on the toes at the curving points; stepping and hopping, hopping up onto a large bowl covered with a sheet of paper, then balancing on the bowl. Kicking one leg forward occurs when the aggressive masculine spirit of General Ch'oe Yŏng has been received.

At various levels, sometimes kneeling on the ground, standing on the bowl, or at an eight-foot height from the ground where the *mudang* balances on knives, the receptive motion of leaning or arching the body backwards becomes the climactic signal of trance-possession. Young shamans are capable of arching based in second position (with legs apart) making a perfect "bridge" backbend; the older ones slant back as far as they can. In this position, the first definite sign of possession occurs with shoulder-quivering, the vibration extending into the arm and hand, eyes closed or fluttering. At grandmother Chŏn's last epic three-day *kut*, before climbing up onto the knives, at ground level, she knelt before the drum, on which she steadied herself with both hands, fiercely shaking her head from side to side, until her head band came off and assisting shamans removed the pins from her hair. Like a young Maenad she tossed her head repeatedly, rapidly up and down, and from side to side in frenzy.

Mostly the patterns consist of walking, and turning as many as twenty times; generally the *mudang* turns to the left, and the *paksu* to the right. Theoretically according to Joseph Campbell, turning to the right winds up the consciousness, turning left unwinds it.[21] In either case, to restore equilibrium, it is usual for the dancer to reverse the turn at some point. Percival Lowell in his book on "Occult Japan"[22] recorded observing the training for trance of the mountain ascetics which consisted in an intensive period of continuous somersaulting around the room first at floor level then off a table ramped on both sides, procedure which would certainly affect the normal flow of blood to the brain. Carmen Blacker's more recent study of shamanist practices in Japan, records feats of levitation where seated shamans rose six or eight inches above the floor in their state of possession.[23] They also jump into the air from the cross-legged position, as sometimes seen in *Noh* and *Kabuki* plays, the technique of which is a secret only possessed by the initiates. If Korean rites are not so acrobatic, they are far more Dionysian, as will be shown.

For dancing measures, clashing cymbals and the strong rhythms of the big drum produce sharp accents; for exalted or emotional states the thin reed pipe or the small trumpet sound piercingly; when the spirit is speaking through the medium of the *mudang's* voice, the two-string viol makes plangent accompaniment. The rhythm patterns of the opening *kŏri* start in slow four-four. As the *kŏri* progress, and intensity rises, rhythms accelerate to the famous six-twelve beat; then the slow and the fast tempi alternate. Dynamically, shaman dancing ranges from soft and light, to sharp, strong, hard accents and tension carried to the point of extreme vibration. Certainly the *mudang* is an astute actress, a dancer of both masculine-feminine styles—the *paksu* too, practices transvestism—and both have compelling expressions to suit the requirements of the different *kut.*

Dionysus in Korea

The fullness of life and the violence of death appeared together as a divine entity, worshipped in Greece in the form of the god Dionysus. The essence of Dionysus is inspiration and intoxication madness, but this madness is not just the temporary or lasting disturbance which can affect mortals, but is rather the companion of life at its healthiest, the madness which attends all moments of creation, and which is particularly inherent in the womb of the mother.[24] Music and dance and prophecy proclaim this fullness of life, which comes to the individual, especially after drinking wine. The priests of Dionysus at Delphi, —whose drink was wine—pronounced oracles long before the Sybilline Apollo pronounced her oracles there. She may have been inspired simply from the vapor coming from the famous cleft in the rock, or perhaps, like her Apollonian peers at Charos, her ecstatic utterance came from drinking holy water. In any case, the later masculine god of light and clarity could not exist without his Dionysian counterpart, the feminine god of darkness and ecstasies. They reigned together at Delphi, in that miraculous flowering of life which the ancient Greeks possessed, because they recognized the essential relatedness of the two natures and permitted one to balance the other.

Dionysus the great god, said to have danced in his mother's womb, is accompanied always by women who are called "nurses." The Bacchoi, or Maenads, are nursing mothers, and in their mad dance following the god, they race through the mountains, with snakes tied in their hair (said to protect them from the lustful attacks of men); they gather up young fawns and wolf cubs and suckle them. But in their manic passion of giving sustenance, they suddenly, destructively change, seize upon the animals, and tear them to pieces. In poetry, vase painting, in sculpture, in Euripides' tragedy of "The Bacchae" the orgiastic scenes have come down to us. For Dionysus is the great god who gives the elixir of life with the shadowing knowledge of the power of death.

Koreans too are noted for their fondness for wine, song and dance. The first mention of Shamanism in *The History of the Three Kingdoms and Oriental Countries*, by the Chinese Jin Su, records: "In Mahan (a country before the Silla dynasty), some festivals took place in May for planting, and in October for harvest, and they have worship for ghosts. The people drink, sing and dance for ten days and night." We can visit most anywhere in the countryside today—away from the modern cement-block city of Seoul—and come upon groups of Koreans—usually women—dancing in the open. They dance unselfconsciously, individually, freely, with that ineluctable sense of *mŏt* and *hŭng* (irrepressible joy from within, state of exhilaration from a deep sense of beauty) which has not changed. Their movements have subtle delicacy, and always that lift of the breath which sends them floating happily over the ground or suspended like a butterfly, on one foot, while the shoulders softly continue to dance. It is this spontaneous, instinctive expression in Korea which I like to call the Lesser Dionysia, and when I think of Korean dancing, the first image which comes to my mind is how untaught countrymen and women naturally express this spirit.

In many shaman ceremonies, a part of the ritual is the *Mugan kŏri* which invites all participating clients to receive the dancing spirit, in a similar outpouring of ecstatic movement. The shaman herself or her assistants encourage each one, selecting costume, robe or hat as appropriate, taking them by the arms, dancing a few steps with them to get them started. Sometimes the shaman herself beats the drum for this festivity. It is fascinating to see individual responses to the opportunity: some dance with eyes completely closed; some go into ecstasy, some into trance. Sometimes, it is reported, they seize flag sticks or props and go about beating things, like the shaman herself. If a person does not dance sufficiently hard enough, the shaman may order them to dance again. Better than any scientifically trained psychiatrist, the shaman knows the needs of her people's psyche and their soma. Here again, the movements are mainly jumping, hopping and turning. Before the privilege of dancing, a thousand *wŏn* note in the city, is usually placed prominently on the altar, on the cow or pig's head.

Most impressive of all is the release of psychic power, and its healing purpose. To see a roomful of women (a few men also) dancing out their various trauma, sharing together the therapeutic experience, is heartening. They are happy to dance with and for their ancestral spirits; in so doing they achieve balance and harmony in their own lives.

Dionysus in Seoul

Usually in spring and autumn, the shamans entertain the spirits, and every ten years or so they entertain their own particular spirits. So May ninth to eleventh this year, grandmother Chŏn in Imun-dong, in the city of Seoul, held a great three day *kut,* marking her seventieth year, and presumably her final chance to welcome and entertain her own special spirits.

The first day was a great feasting celebration like Christmas with the shaman hostess giving gifts of fruit, cakes, towels, and even some money to the guests. Wearing a classical court dancer's hat, with rings on her fingers, necklaces, and a large jade hairpin, grandmother Chŏn sang a welcome song to her spirits, collected money from the guests and after some dancing, an assisting *paksu* (male shaman) officiated in a long service, mostly dancing and turning with fan, scarves, and wands and then giving oracles for two hours.

Pak Man-sin, a young woman assisting shaman, danced with baby clothes, a basket on her head. She threw cakes from the altar into the basket, shook the basket, started jumping, looking happy, sang, and gave a long monologue. She ran three threads from a piece of hemp through her teeth, made a cat's cradle with the last thread, tying a knot, and for two hours gave varied impersonations, some of them comic, talking, singing, dancing. She has a beautiful face, expressive hands and body, excellent mime as a comedienne.

The second morning, all the guests had their individual chance to dance after placing 1,000 *wŏn* notes on the dishes of rice-cakes. The general pattern consisted of rubbing the hands together (a Buddhist adaptation?), walking back and forth, flinging up one sleeve, dancing with arms open, stepping, hopping, turning, climaxed by jumping straight up and down. The flute-player's sister jumped 236 continuous bars of 8 or 1,868 times. The euphoric guests enjoying sips of *makkŏlli,* encourage each other. At the end of each dance, all bow to the spirits' altar, palms together.

In the afternoon, the assisting *paksu* impaled a beautiful skinned and sculpturally white head of an ox onto a trident, which he had first caused to stand upright—a successful sign that the spirits were come. With chanting and cymbal accompaniment, the other shamans bowed before it, then he carried carcasses of the ox and a cow as well as a whole pig through the rooms of the house, and placed them on a wooden platform before the main altar.

The *paksu* performed the *Saeng Tosal Kŏri* (offering of the animals for the spirits). With a hemp-tied stick, he prods and pushes the flesh, and rhythmically thrusts his head toward the meat as he does so. He dances with the ox head, digs into the pig, turns with colored ribbons on a wand, waves the wand over the meat; thrusts the trident into the meat; dances with the scimitar (moonshaped sword), thrusts that into the meat; kisses the blade, makes it balance on a plate in the center of the pig's body. He dances with smaller knives, thrusts them into the meat; alternates dancing and turning with successively smaller sets of knives, and with the long blades upon which grandmother Chŏn ultimately will dance in bare feet. He turns with flags in his hands. Then his sleeves are pulled up and tied behind.

The music has been accelerating to a deafening climax as he suddenly runs through the rooms out into the courtyard, where he picks up a bowl of fresh blood. First smearing some and spews the rest. He takes two pieces of raw meat from a plate, chews and swallows it. Running back into the different rooms, returning outside, he dances again with sets of knives. He ties a white band around his head, dances with hands free; takes up a piece of carcass in his mouth, turns with it, places it on his shoulder, runs through the rooms with it. He does the same with the whole pig, while women follow, mopping up the blood drops. After five turns, a long divination, addressed to grandmother Chŏn, saying — since she is 70 — this is probably the last time she can be present at such a great ceremony, he becomes more and more upset, and turns away, sobbing. All the women are crying.

After he makes the trident balance upright, they hook pieces of carcass onto it. While he sings, people put money on it, and bow to the floor. The ritual is repeated twice more, there is so much meat. Comic reaction when mass of insides starts slipping. He drinks *makkŏlli*. Divines again for grandmother Chŏn; and weeping, she comforts him. All the shamans are refugees from north Korea; all are weeping now for their homeland.

Pak Man-sin performs the next *kut*, dancing with swords, at one time arching backward pointing one sword at her neck, one at her navel. After much jumping, and repeating the backbend, with her hands on her hips, she throws her head from side to side, waves her arms, then holds onto the drum, shaking her head furiously. After singing and dancing, she serves some raw meat to Chŏn and to others. Then she divines with rice grains.

Kim, another assisting shaman, performs similar rites with platters of some by now cooked meat; she dances with first an ox leg on her shoulder; the ribs; another leg; a huge brass bowl of raw cut meat; an aluminum bowl of cooked meat. What together two women can manage to lift of the carcasses they balance on the points of the trident, adding the pig's head with pig's feet put into the pig's mouth, and money placed on top.

The last afternoon, one of the younger shamans performs similar rites, dancing with the ox leg on her shoulder; tosses the leg, kisses it; takes ribs and fat in her arms, onto her shoulders, and turns with it; takes and eats some cooked meat. The inside altar paintings are removed to the courtyard, the altar is set up there, and for a brilliant backdrop, some twenty-seven different shaman costumes hang from a line. For grandmother Chŏn's climactic feat, on top of a large oil-drum they place a table, then a big bowl, on which she will balance standing on the knife edges. First, on the ground, she dances with knives, and divines, telling fortunes with flags. The Spirit Path, a narrow bolt of white cloth, is brought from inside the house-altar to the elevated stand. After hectic head shaking, and vibrating, Chŏn, in trance ascends the stand, holding onto the two long bannered poles. Unsupported at that height, she dances with her arms free; dares to lean backward; faces the North, the East and the North again, chants, sings; at one point, eyes closed, weeping, she wipes her face with the Korean flag on the nearest pole. Up against the sky, balancing successfully, she is secure, in triumph and now, with her spirits, speaks for a long time. Coming down, the Spirit Path unwrapped from around her feet, she sits on a chair talking naturally. Then with General Ch'oe Yŏng's spirit, a sudden shout. She speaks in strong voice, when she sits on a chair. The clients come to her with their skirts held out, for her prophecies made from throwing a few rice grains into their laps. She is Earth Mother, in a general's hat.

Everyone is exhilarated by Chŏn's accomplishment to balance at that high altitude, on the thin blades, and by the total success of her power. After a long pause, the next *Kŏllip Kŏri* (Begging for Offering); the shamans assistants themselves dance a Bacchic revel which becomes a Satyr play. Filled with the new blessings from the spirits, the younger woman shaman and a few others, about six or seven in all, go into the inner altar room, dressing themselves up in pieces of Chŏn's costumes; they tie hemp cloths or twisted towels around their heads; they tuck baby sleeves and jackets into their waist belts, all dancing and laughing at once. Pak Man-sin sings verses, they respond with a chorus, to excited jumping and laughing. After enlarging themselves with half a dozen pieces of costumes each, they pick up and dance with the ox and cow carcasses; one swings the ribs over her head; another carries a whole ox leg outdoors where she turns and whirls with it; one takes ox feet in her hands and makes them dance; finally one Maenad grasps a whole thigh with her teeth in her mouth, and runs out through the gate and into the street beyond with it. Then they stuff food into each other's mouths — rice balls and big bites of pear. One shaman picks up the man helper, carries him piggyback around the rooms; another shaman transfers him to her back.

Grandmother Chŏn, also carried this way, dances with her

arms while being whirled about. While one dances with a cooked chicken on her head, Pak Man-sin, the ringleader, rolls up a piece of paper into a phallic cone, puts it under her skirt, rubs her hips against other women's hips, even grandmother Chŏn's. She throws blankets on the floor, one woman gets under them, and Pak tumbles down on top of her, the two heaving up and down, rolling over and over, and all laughing. The other assisting woman shaman, Kim, usually very sober-faced, puts on make-up: a black mustache, black cheeks and pantomimes comically. Finally Pak Man-sin spins twenty times, performs a somersault, rolls on the floor; dances with wands, whirling, hopping repeatedly on one foot and jumping, for twenty dizzy minutes more.

The final two *kŏri* of this twenty-*kŏri*-long three-day *kut*, served to send the spirits back home, and the tempo slowed down, as it inevitably must. We know the Greek Satyr plays preceded the Dionysian dithyramb, which ultimately became the Greek tragedy ritually performed before the priests of Dionysus and the people of Athens, with the Satyr play coming at the end of the trilogies. Perhaps Korea has the matrix for such a future development into drama — for she has here the basic ingredients: the love of drinking, singing and dancing as the necessary beginning.

Salp'uri

I have been thrilled at the richness of Korean dance, and the final tribute I must pay is to the shaman-derived exorcistic dance known as *salp'uri* (exorcise the evil influences). A solo dance, typically performed by the oldest *mudang*, dressed entirely in white, using a long white scarf, the accompaniment may be the *changgo*, double-barrelled drum, the two stringed viol, (most anciently) the singing voice of the dancer, or the *kayagŭm*, the ancient plucked instrument with its vibratory shaking notes like suppressed sobbing.

It is subtle, full of suspensions, the motion held back, then bursting out with surprising flicks of the scarf; teasing, capricious, rapturous, with improvisational impulses, and magnetic command of the body. Here Dionysus himself is captured, subdued, entertained, and sent away, as in no other dance.

I have been privileged to see some of Korea's treasury of dance forms, unequalled in Asia, as they flower in the elegant femininity of the court dances; the passionate feeling of the Buddhist dances with their magnificent drumming; the exuberant farmers dance, and supremely, the shaman dance of the spirit. As Dionysians, the have known and cherished the dance as the vital link to the divine spirit. Here is the true and secret power of Korean dance.

Unfortunately, the present government considers Shamanism mere superstition. It does everything to discourage it, and in fact, since 1975 the practice of Shamanism is now banned in Cheju Island. This is a discouraging portent for the rest of the country, where it is estimated, there may be as many as 10,000 shaman practitioners, (no one really knows how many there are). After a four year intensive study of Shamanism by a current member of Korea's board of psychiatry, the psychiatrist conceded that while there may be "a projective tendency in Shamanism which encourages paranoia among its clients," his conclusion was a positive one: from the humanist point of view, the shaman stands on the side of humanity and for therapeutic alleviation of human suffering.

The future of Shamanism — so deep a part of the fabric of Korean life — faces ineluctable 'progress' in a world made safe for real estate operators; in the electronic age where ordinary time and space boundaries are abolished with the turn of a dial, the sacred realm of the spirits recedes more and more. Shamanism has withstood hundreds of years of opposition; before it disappears, may Koreans continue to appreciate and at least record what they have, for theirs is unique in the world.

NOTES

1. The recent fourth study to Japan and first visit to Bali undertaken with a much-appreciated grant from the Vogelstein Foundation.
2. Yoshimaro Hanayagi, classical dancer, Kyoto, Japan.
3. *Dance Perspectives* 19, New York 1964.
4. Laurel Kendall: "To my knowledge the Confucius ceremony is done in Taiwan but far less 'authentically.' Each year costumes of different dynasties are worn."
5. Sŏng Kyŏng-rin, "Korean Classic Dance," *Korea Journal* Vol. 3 No. 2 (1963 February) p. 6.
   Bugaku were imported to Japan after *Gigaku*.
6. Alan C. Heyman, *Ibid.* p. 10.
7. Sŏng Kyŏng-rin, (in Korean) "Dance In Korea." Former Director National Classical Music Institute. Association for Memorial for King Sejong. Seoul. 1976. p. 124 Trans. by Pak Sang-wŏn.
8. Alan Heyman. *Ibid.* p. 27
9. Yi Tu-hyŏn, (Lee Du-hyun) "Korean Mask-Dance Drama," Research Institute of Korean Mask-Dance Drama. 1975.
10. Yi Tu-hyŏn, *Traditional Performing Arts of Korea*, Korean National Commission for UNESCO, 1975. p. 367.
11. *"Kugak Kaeron,"* (Introduction to Korean Music). Chang Sa-hun and Han Man-yŏng, Seoul National College of Music. 1975. pp. 176–80/trans. Pak Sang-wŏn.
12. Fr. Sean Dwan, dissertation, "Shamanism," Yonsei Uni. Oct. 1976.
13. Suanne Langer, *Feeling and Form*, Scribner. 1965.
14. Yi Tu-hyŏn, "Characteristics of Korean Shamanism." 1976.
15. Alan C. Heyman, *Ibid*, p. 25.
16. Yu Tong-shik, "The World of *Kut* and Korean Optimism." *Korea Journal*. Vol. 13 August '73.
17. Source: Dr. Yun Sun-yŏng, Ewha Womans University.
18. Curt Sachs, *The World History of the Dance*, Norton, New York. 1938.
19. Mircea Eliade, *Shamanism: The Archaic Technique of Ecstasy*, Pantheon. 1964.
20. Otaker Pertold, "The Ceremonial Dance of the Sinhales, An Inquiry into Sinhales Folk Religion." Sri Lanka. *The Ceylon Historical Journal*, Volume Twenty. Reprinted 1973. first printed 1930 p. 17.
21. Joseph Campbell, "The Masks of God," *Oriental Mythology*, Viking Press. 1967.
22. Percival Lowell, *Occult Japan*, Boston. 1895.
23. Carmen Blacker, *The Catalpa Bow, A Study of Shamanist Practice in Japan*, London, Allen & Unwin. 1975.

24. Walter F. Otto, *Dionysus, Myth and Cult,* Indiana University Press, Bloomington and Londin. 1965. pp. 143–5.
25. Kim Kwang-il "Shamanist Healing Ceremonies in Korea." *Korea Journal,* April 1973. p. 47.

Moving in the Korean Way:

Movement Characteristics of the Korean People as Expressed in Their Dance

CHRISTINE LOKEN

In this paper, I will deal with the basic elements of Korean dance, how the dancer uses his or her body and how this reflects the movement patterns of the culture as a whole. These elements run through all forms of Korean dance and form its unique movement profile.

I am starting from the assumption that dance is a unique form of cultural expression, as it deals with the very body image of its people. Dance, being dependent on one's physical body for expression, has necessarily developed to take into account the strengths and weaknesses of its people. The build, proportions and suppleness of the body determine to a great extent the nature of the dance form, and these are dependent on a combination of factors: genetic, dietary, climatic, environmental and social. All of these factors must be taken into consideration when we look for subliminally predominant movement patterns within a culture.

It is my contention that these movement patterns do exist and that it is these subliminal patterns which have traditionally been exaggerated and expressed through dance, making it at once recognizable and acceptable to people within that culture. These patterns may be in the form of patterns for energy use; so that one culture may have a tendency for burst-sustain movements, while another may perform movements in the more isolated fashion of continual small bursts. Or they may surface as a tendency for isolation or unity of body parts, or a tendency for flat or curved movement through space.

Historically we know that dancers have travelled between different countries, taking their dances with them and teaching them to the people of their host country. Yet in adopting a new dance style. I feel that the people of a culture can only adopt that which is already in accord with their own values and body structure, and so certain changes take place in the dance until it is acceptable to its new owners.

We know that dance movements and themes traveled out of India to influence the dance cultures of every other Asian country. And that China was also a powerful influence for both Korea and Japan. Yet in the end we have movement styles which are each very different and easily identified. And each country ends up with a dance form which it considers to be "natural". This feeling of the "naturalness" of a dance form to the people of its culture is very strong. In some ways this is obvious; the costume may be similar to the dress worn in daily life, such as in Korea where the dancers wear *hanbok*. The relationships between people of varied status may be shown conforming to the relationships within that society, as in Korea where we see stress on the proper behavior between people and the five relationships of the Confucian Classics: ruler and subject, husband and wife, father and son, older and younger brother, and friend and friend, depicted either in their proper or improper forms.

In other ways it may reach so deeply that it speaks directly to the person's subconscious, because, "there is no other way that it could be." This is the area which encompasses: the definition of joints and body units, characteristic shapes, continuous or broken movement, density of movement, use of time, motivation force, use of the hand and face, posture, characteristic walk, center of weight, and flow of energy.

The particular "naturalness" of Korean dance is brought about because rather than isolating various parts of the body as dancers in some cultures do, in Korean dance there is one central impetus for the movement and the whole body moves along the curve of this flow.

This curve or moving line is a central theme of Korean dance and Korean traditional life, and one which you can see in every dance that you view. It is important to realize, however, that this curve in space is never a static position but rather the constant creation of the curve through movement. Instead of using the curve as a shape, in contrast to straight lines or angles, the Korean dancer is never still, but always moving, always creating new curves in space, whether through movements of the whole body, the arm, the shoulders, or the line of the costume. For example, we see in the line of the sleeve a curve which is emphasized by the movements of the arm, and the skirt constantly whirls out or around the body forming new circles. *Hansam*, long sleeves which extend over the wrists, are used in court and masked dances, and are either gently or vigorously swung about to create curves. Streamers, *ch'ae sang*, are attached to the hats of the hand drum, *sogo*, players in the farmers, bands. These streamers are about six feet long and rotate by means of a stiff rope looped around a swivel at the top of the hat.

We can see curves everywhere in Korean traditional society: the line of the roof, the clothing's sleeves and pants, the peach shape of the buttons, the Korean sock and shoe, the hills and mountains, the rice fields, and the age-old gesture of even the most modern Korean in pouring your drink.

Korean dance has essentially a kinetic rather than a sculptural quality. The dancer is never still, something is always moving and this basic quality alone makes it appear graceful and gentle. The economy of movement and its delicacy, together with the generally slow rhythms, give the dance a low movement density. But then, the audience is not watching for technical virtuosity but rather to see if the dancer has the "spirit" of the dance, the joy and ecstasy, *mŏt* and *hŭng*.

The Koreans seek the infinite and eternal in the eternal flow of life, the constancy of the continual change from yin to yang. In Korean dance the interrelatedness of the whole; arms to chest, chest to breathing, breathing to tension and relaxation, and this, reflected back in the movement of the hands, makes the whole seem to revolve like the eternally changing yin and yang, moving from dark to light, or, more appropriately, from heavy to light.

This feeling of heaviness, *mugŏpta*, is an important aspect of Korean dance, especially the classical style. Although in neighboring Japan the dance also has a stress on heaviness, for the Japanese this is a downward force which represents a sense of settledness, *ochitsuita*, of immoveability or stability. In Korean dance, however, we feel this as a rejuvenating force, something which the dancer uses to rise again.

The interrelatedness of body parts is exactly what makes it so intangible and difficult to master and also what accounts for the slight variation in movement and timing whenever a group of dancers performs together. These variations tend to blur the edges of the movement and give it an even softer appearance. The dancer seems to flow on with everything moving at once. There are no poses or positions that one can, or should, fix upon. And the soft, relaxed quality is impossible to strive for, since the more effort you put into it the more elusive it seems to be. The only solution in this case is to let the spirit dance. Since Shamanism, as influenced by Taoist and Buddhist practices, is the basis for Korean indigenous art, this seems to be a good idea, indeed.

Let's look at the Korean use of the hand. Koreans, especially the women, seem to have somewhat rounded hands. The back of the hand is rather fleshy and there is a softness over the knuckles. The wrist is not usually boney so the line of the arm extends almost unbroken to the end of the hand. I think these characteristics must be heightened by diet and climate since the Koreans that I have met in America do not exhibit this to such a great extent.

I feel, after observing both the dance and daily movements of Koreans, that they experience the hand as a single unit. There is not a great deal of definition of the finger joints while gesturing. Where some cultures tend to grab space, Koreans tend to slice through it. Koreans also tend to leave their hands in a relaxed state as much as possible and avoid highly articulated gestures; so when holding on to bus rails or another person's arm they often leave the thumb in line with the fingers and only slightly cup the tips of the fingers, instead of wrapping the fingers and thumb completely around. When turning the page of a book, they lay the hand flat on the surface of the page and catch the page by opening and closing the space between the second and third or third and fourth fingers instead of taking the corner of the page between the thumb and first finger. And when indicating something, they tend to keep their second finger extended and slightly cup the others instead of isolating the first finger and folding the other fingers into a fist at the base of it.

Within the dance too, we can see this relaxed attitude of the hand. The hand is an extension of the whole arm and never a separate, isolated entity. The fingers do not articulate or form gestures in any way.

In many of the Asian dance forms the hands are used to form intricate gestures which communicate the narrative story of the dance. This is not true in Korea. Korean dance essentially expresses the mood or spirit of the dancer rather than a story. This relaxed hand is a unique characteristic of Korean dance. In both neighboring China and Japan, although the physical characteristics of the people are quite similar, a gesture language has developed. In China, by using the sleeve and holding the hand in various positions while speaking, and in Japan, by using the fan. The Japanese use of the hand is extremely refined and subtle, and while they also tend to move the hand as a single unit, keeping the fingers together, the movement is of a sequential nature and ends in an extended, somewhat convex position. Very different from the rounded and relaxed position found in Korean dance.

The face is kept in a seemingly relaxed state and the eyes are slightly lowered, but in fact, while the dancer does not articulate his or her face in any way, a subtle shifting of emotion seems to express itself through its calm and placid exterior. With a good dancer, we can feel the controlled passion, the ecstasy, which swells up from within during the dance, the *mŏt* and *hŭng*. So also in society we find that the Confucian ideal is emotional control and physical non-expression, while the people tend to be very emotional and romantic.

Just as we can find similarities between the Korean use of the hand and face in daily life and in dance, we can also make observations about posture and walking style. If you observe Koreans in the street you will notice that they walk tall with an easy and relaxed stride. They tend to walk or stand with their toes turned slightly out and the chest lifted. They walk robustly and confidently in a single direction and as a single block, yet have an amazing way of slipping or sliding by things. They seem to have their eyes on some distant goal and to wind their way down the street toward it.

In dance the Koreans step forward with heel meeting the ground first and the toes turned up. This movement is emphasized by the line of the Korean sock which is turned up at the toe and curved at the heel. The aesthetic is to pad the foot so that it looks plump and round and the heel looks like an egg. They also turn on their heels and run by gliding along heel first. While this is now a stylized movement, it does come from a natural walk.

We would expect to find this same sense of interrelatedness and integration of body parts and energy flow in the walk that we find in the shoulders and arms. The Korean dancer proceeds through space in a curve, sometimes even, and sometimes varied.

If we compare this line to other East Asian walking styles, we find that each is distinctly different. The Chinese lift at the beginning and then swoop down and the Japanese drop down and then move straight along or gradually rise in a controlled way. The Koreans, as mentioned before, roll along gently.

Another aspect of Korean life which we find in stylized form in the dance is the squat. In Korea, because of the fullness of the traditional clothing, the squat is a broad one, with the knees usually at least shoulder width apart. In the folk dances the dancer may jump into this squat position and out again into the air. I feel that this particular movement illustrates the connections between Korean and Mongolian and Central Asian dance.

Next, let's look at the use of the torso and the center of weight. In general, I feel that Koreans do not use their bodies as a conglomeration of many separate parts, which can be manipulated individually, but rather as a group of single units. In other words, the torso is perceived of as one unit, the head as one, each arm as one, and each leg as one. These units bend and fold in the same way that a string may bend as we bring the two ends together, but they do not break into various distinct angles. Koreans do not isolate the pelvis, the knee joints, the head or the shoulders. The shoulder dancing, *okkae-ch'um*, of Korea is a sequential movement rather than an isolated one, and comes from a lift in the upper chest. After observing Korean dancers and people in daily life, it is my opinion that they perceive their center of weight as being in their upper chest or lung area.

Koreans tend, when walking, to lift their chests and let the rest of the torso move freely underneath. With the men this emphasis on the chest area often takes the form of a modified *yangban* or nobleman's walk. With women you find that the chest area is held somewhat thickly with the arms slightly forward. Their shoulders tend to be full and rounded, rather than angular. In dance this emphasis on the chest area takes the form of a concave position of the upper torso, a position that allows the jacket, *chŏgori*, to lie flat on the skirt, *ch'ima*.

On the basis of extended observation, I conclude that within

Korean philosophy the fact that breath is linked to the *ki* (氣) or spirit, is partially responsible for this emphasis on the chest and lung areas. And that this way of relating to *ki* as breath is closely tied with the use of breath to initiate movement. We can see in both Korean female dance styles and masked dance that the movement of the shoulders or the torso is a manifestation of the focus on the upper chest and rib cage as the area which relates to breathing. The cycle created by following the natural breathing cycle can also be seen as an interplay between tension and relaxation. As the dancer breathes in, the chest lifts and expands in an energetic way, and the wave of energy flows out through the arms in a sequential movement. Then, when the dancer exhales the chest sinks and the wave goes out again in reverse. This interplay between energy and relaxation, or tension and relaxation can be seen continually in Korean daily life. Koreans seem to alternate between periods of extremely high energy and total relaxation. The alternation between tension and relaxation is something which is very Korean and difficult for Westerners to master. Since we are used to maintaining one constant level of tension rather than dropping in and out of it at regular intervals, we tend to look for positions into which we can move our bodies. But as previously stated, there are no positions, the dancer is continually moving, caught in the flow of life, breath, tension and relaxation.

With breath playing such an important and integral part in the phrasing of the dance, it is not surprising that Korean dance has an ecstatic quality. For centuries, people have honored the importance of breath and have realized that by the manipulation of breath certain states of altered consciousness could be achieved. Perhaps this is part of the Korean shaman's technique for entering her trance state. With this in mind, it is interesting to note again that dancers are judged on their *mŏt* and *hŭng*, joy and ecstasy, rather than for their technique, and that their faces seem to radiate with some inner glow.

In summary, the main characteristics of Korean dance are: emphasis on the moving curve, economy and delicacy of movement giving it a low movement density, body parts used as units rather than highly articulated, relaxed quality of the hand, rolling walk, stepping and turning heel-first, jumping in and out of a squat position, center of weight in the upper chest, breath as an integral force in the dance, sequential movements with impetus in the upper chest, emphasis on mood, ecstasy and joy, rather than story line.

NOTES

1. Lomax Alan, *Folk Songs Style and Culture*, (Washington D.C., AAAS Pub. No. 88, 1968)
2. Loken, Christine, "An Exploration Study of Breath as an Aesthetic Consideration in Asian Dance," UCLA M.A. Thesis, 1974, p. 4.
3. Van Zile, Judy, "Energy Use," presented at the CORD Conference (San Fransisco, 1974)
4. Hutchinson, Ann, *Labanotation, The System of Analyzing and Recording Movement,* revised and expaned ed., (New York, Theatre Arts, 1976)
5. King, Eleanor, "Reflections on Korean Dance," *Korea Journal* (Aug., 1977), pp. 36–55.
6. Heyman, Alan, "Dance of the Three Thousand League Land," *Dance Perspectives,* No. 19 (New York, 1964)
7. Kendall, Laurel, "Mugum: The Dance in Shaman's Clothing," *Korean Journal,* Vol. 17 No. 12 (Dec., 1977), pp. 38–44.
8. Lee Du-hyun, *Korean Mask Dance Drama,* (Seoul, Research Institute of Mask Dance Drama, 1975)

Crane Dances in Korea

CHRISTINE LOKEN

The crane is a symbol often used in both court and folk art in Korea. For centuries the Manchurian and white napped cranes have stopped over in Korea on their yearly migrations. In recent years they have been settling temporarily in an estuary on the Han River near the demilitarized zone. They are also spotted sometimes in the south of Korea in South Kyŏngsang Province, along the stretch of land between the Nakdong River and Chinju town.

In Korea, as well as in China and Japan, the crane is a symbol of longevity. In Korea, we often find it represented in the *sip changsaeng* (ten long life symbols) design which appears on screens, pillow ends, spoon-bags, brush holders, ink stones, quivers, pottery, tea tables, coins, chests, and scrolls.[1] As one of the ten long life symbols, the crane appears with the pine, turtle, deer, bamboo, *pulloch'o* (herb of immortality), rock, water, cloud and sun. The crane is also the symbol of peace, purity and simplicity, since it picks its way through the muddy waters of rivers, catches edible things in its beak, washes them in the water and throws away the ones that are not good. So the crane has come to be a reminder of how the righteous person should also go through his life selecting the pure and moral way and rejecting the bad and immoral.

In Korea, another frequently seen symbol is the lotus. To the Buddhists, the lotus is a symbol of enlightenment, since it grows up through the muddy waters of the pond and blossoms clear and bright on the surface. It symbolizes the conquest of worldly evils and temptations and the rising above them to retain only the pure. The court crane dance grew out of Yŏnhwa-dae, the lotus flower dance, and as we see, they are connected through their philosophical symbolism.

Another way in which the crane was used as a symbol in Korea, was on the *hyungbae*, parapet, worn on the front and back of the civil officials' costumes during the Yi dynasty (1392-1910). A pair of cranes carrying the herb of immortality in their mouths and surrounded by multi-colored clouds, waves and rocks was embroidered on the *hyungbae* of upper level civil officials and a single crane in the same setting was embroidered on the *hyungbae* of lower level civil officials.

There are at present two distinct types of crane dance in Korea. In one, the dancer wears a feathered costume with an extended neck and black stockings, realistically depicting a crane. In the other, the dancer wears a white cotton *top'o*, a long traditional man's coat with square sleeves over *paji* or pants, and *chŏgori* or jacket. A *kat*, a high black horsehair hat, is also worn. In recent times, both of these types have existed as folk forms. Korea has not had an active court since 1910, when the Japanese annexed the country, and the National Classical Music Institute, whose job it is to preserve the court dances and music, no longer performs the crane dances.[2]

The dance type in which the dancer wears a feathered crane costume is found in Seoul area and occasionally in dance studios throughout the country. It is modeled after the *Hang-mu*, crane dance, of the Yi dynasty court. The title *Hang-mu* comes from the Chinese characters; *hak* (鶴) representing crane, and *mu* (舞) representing dance. *Ch'um* is the pure Korean word for dance, so from now on the words *Hang-mu* will be used to refer to the dance in the feathered costume, and the words *hak-ch'um* will be used to refer to the folk versions performed in traditional Korean clothes. Although, as was previously stated, both types are technically "folk" versions now.

The oldest written record that we have of the *Hang-mu* are

Kim Tŏk-myŏng in a dance pose from the *Yangsan Hakch'um.*

found in the *Akhak kwebŏm*, a treatise on music and dance written in 1493 during the 24th year of King Sŏng-jong's reign of the Yi dynasty. This book contains a record of the instruments, costumes, properties, and number of players and some choreographic and other information relevant to the study of dance and music. Another book, *Chinyon ŭi Kwe* gives the dates and occasions of performances during the Yi dynasty. In the *Akhak kwebŏm*, the dance is divided into *Hyang-ak chŏngjae*, dance originating in Korea, and *Tang-ak chŏngjae*, dance derived from China. According to the *Akhak kwebŏm*, there were either *Hyang-ak chŏngjae* being performed at that time, one of these was *Hang-mu* and another *Hak Yŏnhwadae Ch'ŏyong hapsŏl*, a dance which combined the dance of the crane, the lotus (*yŏnhwa*), and a dance to the five directions (*ch'ŏyong mu*). These dances are classified as *Hyang-ak* because at the start of the dance the music started and the dance began without any signal words or song as was the case in the *Tang-ak* pieces.³ The dances were all accompanied by songs from the Koryŏ or Sŏn-ch'o periods and *Hang-mu* used the music *Pohŏjaryŏng*.⁴

As mentioned above, the dance *Hak Yŏnhwadae Ch'ŏyong hapsŏl* was really a combination of dances and quite a large scale event. As such, it followed the all night shaman ceremony, *Na Rye*, and came to be divided into two parts. The first section contained the *Ch'ŏyong* dance and singing, and the second part contained several dances. According to the *Akhak kwebŏm*, in the second part the players sang *Yŏngsan hoesang pul bosal*, then the big drum (*puk*) sounded and the musicians played *Yŏngsan hoesang ryong*. When the rhythm quickened, the *Obang Ch'ŏyong* (dancers to the five directions) began to dance, they were followed by some *yŏgi* (dancing girls) and musicians and small masked dancing boys. After that the players danced the *Hang-mu* to the music *Pohŏjaryŏng*. In the dance the cranes discovered two little girls hidden in lotus flowers located on the dance area and these little girls came out and danced *Yŏnhwa-dae chŏngjae*. Next the group sang the second part of *Ch'ŏyong-ga* (the *Ch'ŏyong song*). After that, they ended the performance by singing three Buddhist songs of appreciation. At the end of the Yi dynasty all of these dances were lost.⁴

The first written record of *Hang-mu* is found in the *Akhak kwebŏm* in connection with the dance *Yŏnhwa-dae*. *Yŏnhwa-dae*, however, is first mentioned in the *Koryŏ-sa Ak chi*, the section of the chronicles of the Koryŏ period (918-1392) which deals with music and dance. According to the *Koryŏ-sa Ak chi*, after an introductory song, the two little girls came out of the lotuses and danced. Although they danced to a piece of music entitled "White Crane" no cranes appeared to discover the young girls.⁵ In the *Akhak kwebŏm*, there is notation for both *Hang-mu* and *Yŏnhwadae*, showing that they were each fully developed and independent, though often interlocking dances. The *Hang-mu* of the *Akhak kwebŏm* has two cranes, a blue one (on the east) and a white one (on the west), the traditional color for each direction. Toward the end of the Yi dynasty, another book was written giving specific instructions about the dance, *Kungjung chŏngjae-mu toholgi* (the version consulted dates at perhaps 1893). At that time the two cranes wore yellow and blue. The blue crane was still on the east side, but on the west there was then a yellow crane instead of a white one. The music they used at this later date was *Ch'aeŭn sŏnhak chi-gok.*

The description of the dance is almost exactly the same in the two books. In both, the King was sitting in the north and the cranes were dancing between him and the lotus pond (a platform with two lotuses attached to it and other simulated rocks and trees) in the south. The dance takes twenty-three measures in both versions and there is only slightly more description in the *Akhak kwebŏm* (there are instructions specifying beginning on the right foot, for example). The cranes entered from the sides and faced north in the beginning. They shook their bodies and beaks and began to dance; taking two steps and then looking in, and two steps and then looking out, and moving back and forth to the north and south. They moved back and forth between the king and the lotus pond several times, occasionally stopping to shake their feathers, and finally went over and pecked at the lotus so that it opened revealing two young girls. The cranes jumped back in surprise and then withdrew as the next dance began.[6]

The dance was probably performed for the edification of the king and in hopes that it would bring peace to his mind.[7] After 1902, however, it was lost.[8] In 1935, it was recreated by Han Sŭng-jun (1874-1941) a famous folk dancer. He created a new *Hang-mu* based on the court dance. The costume used presently is somewhat different from the pictures found in the *Akhak kwebŏm*, and is only black and white, but is still realistic in approach. His granddaughter, Han Yŏung-suk, has been designated a National Cultural Treasure for her rendition of this dance and the crane costume. At the present time the *Hang-mu* may be seen at various performance, often

in connection with a version of *Yŏnhwa-dae*. It has moved into
the realm of folk dance and is thus open to interpretation by
many choreographers.

The second type of crane dance found in Korea is the *Hak-
ch'um* done in traditional Korean dress. There are two versions
of this dance, *Tongnae Hak-ch'um* and *Yangsan Hak-ch'um*,
both from the South Kyŏngsang Province. Tongnae was a
village near the port city of Pusan and Yangsan is a mountain
near there. Both of these dances are what might be termed
traditional folk dance in that they were handed down from
one generation to the next, usually within the same family. At
present, there is one person maintaining the dance in each
form.

As with all folk arts, we have little in the way of written
records of these dances. Several years ago Prof. Sŏ Kuk-yŏng of
Pusan National University carried out some research on these
dances and gathered informations from the dancers and older
people who had played some part in their histories.

In earlier times, the Tongnae area was a stopping place for
cranes on their yearly migration. In Yŏnsan-dong, southwest
of Tongnae, there was a large pond called Mudinggi-mot. This

Yi Hyŏn-gyŏng in dance poses from the *Tongnae Hak-ch'um*

pond was often filled with cranes. In the center of the pond there was a large rock called Taejo-am (large bird rock) because the cranes often landed there. In recent years the pond had dried up and the cranes no longer come to Tongnae, however, the rock remains.

Behind Tongnae village there is a hill which reminded the people of a crane, so different parts of it were named after the parts of a crane; Haksudae (the neck of the crane), Haksodae (the nest of the crane), Ma-annyŏng (the body of the crane), Tongjang-dae (the left, east, wing of the crane) and Sŏjang-dae (the right, west, wing of the crane). On Sŏjang-dae was located the chŏgch'ui chŏng, a house where folk musicians performed and had contests, and village people came to enjoy their songs and dances.

Near the pond, Mudinggi-mot, there was a village named Hwangsae-al (big bird's egg) and at Ma-am-kol (horse blanket valley) there was a dance practice place. This was just below the present Kŭmjang park where practice sessions for the current Tongnae groups are held.[9] It is not known how long ago these areas first became known by crane related names. The earliest written record is from 1867-9 when the Tongnae governor, Chŏn Hyŏn-dŏk, then in the process of establishing a military, noted in his records that weapons were being produced at Haksu-dae.[10]

Cranes then were a frequent sight in the Tongnae area, and it is not surprising that the people of Tongnae created a dance in celebration of the elegant movements of these birds. The *Tongnae hak-ch'um* was the product of an old men's society in Tongnae, organized by retired officials of the upper class, or *yangban*. These officials settled in Tongnae toward the end of the Yi dynasty. In 1953, forty-four such officials gathered to organize the first *Ki-yŏng-kye*. A *Chwamok* or book giving the members' names, group rules and aims, was written by Mun Chin-yŏl, in the same year.[11] One of the articles said that at the spring meeting every year they would have a *pabsang-norŭm*, an offering of food and wine to the parents of the men.

This was a way of paying respects to their elders and was supposed to be followed by singing and dancing. It was at this occasion that the crane dance came to be performed.

The first crane dancer whose name has come down to us is Yi Chu-sŏ, who danced from 1907 (when the original *Ki-yŏng-kye* became the *Ki-yŏng-hŭi*) until 1920.

In 1915, another group was established in Tongnae, the *mang-sun-kye*, to which men of the *sŏmin* class belonged. This group held four meetings a year. In April and October their meetings involved some kind of ritual celebration. These rituals also included dancing and music since the Tongnae people had long been famous as good dancers and musicians. From 1915-1940, three people danced the *Hak-ch'um* at these celebrations; Kim Kui-cho, Kim P'il-sang (not a member of the society) and Ch'oe Sun-baek. Of these three, Kim Kui-cho (1888-1956) was recognized as the best dancer.

Although Kim Kui-cho never studied from Yi Chu-sŏ, it is believed that he observed his dancing and was able to duplicate Mr. Yi's poses with only this brief exposure. The crane was so popular with the members of the *mang-sun-kye*, that soon it came to the attention of the Tongnae masked dance players. The Tongnae players approached Kim Kui-cho and asked him to perform the dance as an introductory presentation at the masked dance performances. This he agreed to do and thus the *Tongnae hak-ch'um* and the *Tongnae yayu* (field play) began to be performed together.[12] Kim Kui-cho taught his dance to his son Kim Hŭi-yŏng, and died in 1956, leaving him to carry on the tradition. Kim Hŭi-yŏng is not recognized as having been an outstanding perpetuator of this tradition because of his weak physical condition and he died in October 1972. During his last year, he taught the dance to his niece, Yi Hyŏn-gyŏng, then a girl of thirteen. She has maintained it under the watchful eyes of Mun Chang-wŏn and the other *Tongnae yayu* players and is now the perpetuator of this dance. Since 1976, it has been performed with five players, Miss Yi and four men. In the beginning of the dance, the four men circle the stage. They dance together and then separate to form a square into which Miss Yi dances. From that point on she does the dance as it was taught to her by her uncle with the four men framing her movements. Several times during the dance they join with her in dancing the *ttotbaegi* step — a hop into a lunge position.

The dance is performed to the *kutkŏri* rhythm, a 4/4 rhythm in triplets or 12/8. Played on the *changgo* (hourglass shaped drum), *ching* (gong), *puk* (barrel shaped drum), and *kkwaeng-gari* (a small gong). In the dance of Kim Hŭi-yŏng there were 67 measures.[13]

In the Tongnae dance there are ten movements: flying (entrance), landing, enjoying flying, stretching after flying *(ttotbaegi)*, standing on one leg and hopping, small jumps, looking for food, picking up food and flying (exit).[14] The dance is basically abstract with most of the attention on the dance movements rather than on the movements which pantomime crane actions. The two main dance movements which are repeated throughout the dance from various positions on the dance space are; *ttotbaegi*, a jump, followed by a hop on the right foot with the left foot swinging across to the right, and then swinging out for a lunge to the left front diagonal, and *olimsae*, flying movements with the arms alternately swinging up above the head and down by the ear. During the dance the hands are often extended palm down from the wrist with the fingers spread representing the feathers at the tips of the crane's wings. The costume enhances the abstract quality since the white coat with large sleeves and the black hat merely suggest the coloring and physical shape of the crane.

The *Yangsan hak-ch'um* is said to have originated in Tongdo-sa, a temple located on Yang Mountain. It is one of the largest temples in Korea and unfortunately in 1945, at the end of the Japanese occupation of Korea, the temple was racked with internal disorder. All of its records were destroyed so that we are unable to substantiate stories of the *Hak-ch'um* originating there. It is said that the *Hak-ch'um* was danced by monks in gray *changsam*, or robe, with the red *kasa*, a square cloth worn over the shoulder, and *kkokkal*, the peaked Buddhist hat.[15] It is said that in the 1880s, Kim Tu-sik of Tong myŏng, Naesŏng-ri, began dancing the *Hak-ch'um*. He often went up to Tongdo-sa Temple to carry rice and grain down to the Tongnae village and it is believed that he had the opportunity to see the monk Yi Wŏl-ho dancing. Kim Tu-sik was in charge of the local dancers in Naesŏng-ri village and he taught the crane dance to Hwang Chong-yŏl, 1887-1957, who later taught it to Kim Tŏk-myŏng, Kim Tu-sik's grandson. Kim Tŏk-myŏng is now the perpetuator of this dance.[16]

In the *Yangsan hak-ch'um* the music is *kutkŏri* as in the *Tongnae* version, and the musical instruments used are the same. There are fourteen basic movements; flying (entrance), landing, looking for danger, searching for food, playing joyfully, picking up food, washing and shaking the food, resting in the sun, looking at another crane teasingly, walking in front of another crane and leading it, feeding food to another crane, two cranes playfully touching, walking and looking for a direction to fly, flying (exit).[17]

By looking over this list of dance movements, we can see that the emphasis is on a realistic portrayal of the crane's actions. The *Yangsan hak-ch'um* is thus much more concrete than the *Tongnae hak-ch'um* and in that way is closer to the court dance in quality. Looking at the three versions of the crane dance; the court crane dance is concrete in both costume and actions and the Tongnae crane dance is abstract in both costume and actions. The Yangsan crane dance lies somewhere in-between, with an abstract costume and concrete pantomimed actions.

At present the two forms of the *Hak-ch'um* are presented only occasionally. The *Tongnae hak-ch'um* is no longer attached to the elder men's society and is now seen only in connection with the *Tongnae yayu* or when performances are specially requested. It has been designated a Pusan city cultural treasure and as such it receives official support for its continued preservation and is occasionally presented in folk festivals and competitions, or to groups of older citizens or school children. Performances of the *Yangsan hak-ch'um* are somewhat rarer, since Yangsan is located outside of Pusan city and the *Yangsan hak-ch'um* does not have that official support. Just as the cranes themselves are in danger of extinction and are currently being protected by a society set up for that purpose, the crane dances have lost something of their vitality and the support of city or national cultural organizations plays some role in their survival. The village of Tongnae is now part of Pusan city and is no longer a stopping place for cranes on their yearly migrations, and the people of Tongnae are no longer awed and thrilled by the sight of these great birds. As citizens of a large modern city they are also exposed to television, movies and other forms of entertainment, and live performances of the traditional dances may not be looked forward to in quite the same manner that they were in the years before such mass entertainment was available. The country's cultural organizations are helping to counteract that trend somewhat as with their support the dances are reaching greater audiences through appearances in festivals and on television. So perhaps the dances are about to enter a new phase, where they mean somewhat less to a greater number of people.

NOTES

1. Zo Za-yong, *The Flavor of Korean Folk Painting*, (Seoul, Korea: Encyclopedia Britannica, 1972), p. 25.
2. Kim Ch'ŏn-hŭng, June 11, 1978, discussion at the Korean National Classical Music Institute.
3. Chang Sa-hun, *Han'guk Chŏnt'ong Muyong Yŏn'gu* (A Study on Traditional Korean Dances), (Seoul, Korea: Ilchisa, 1977), p. 57.
4. Han Ok-hŭi, July 12, 1978, as per her examination of the *Chinyon ŭi Gwe.*

5. Ch'a Chu-hwan, translator, *Koryŏ-sa Akchi,* (Seoul, Korea: Ūlyu-munhwa-sa 93, 1972), p. 298.
6. Chang Sa-hun, *op. cit.* p. 191 and 258.
7. Kim Ch'ŏn-hŭng, June 11, 1978.
8. Han Ok-hŭi, July 12, 1978, as per her examination of the *Chinyon ŭi Gwe.*
9. Sŏ Kuk-yŏng and Kim Ch'ŏn-hŭng, *"Tongnae hak-ch'um,"* A Report of Research on the Intangible Cultural Treasures. Vol. 105 (Seoul, Korea; Bureau of Cultural Properties Management, 1972).
10. *Ibid.*
11. *Ibid.*
12. *Ibid.*
13. *Ibid.*
14. *Ibid.*
15. Sŏ Kuk-yŏng, *Sach'al (Yangsan) hak-ch'um,* A Report of Research on the Intangible Cultural Treasures Vol. 122, 1976.
16. *Ibid.*
17. *Ibid.*

Farmers Music and Dance

KIM YANG-GON

This research is conducted with the aim of exploring the possibility of applying the music and dance of Korea's farmers to formal education so that students can be encouraged to deepen their knowledge of the nation's unique cultural heritage. It is necessary for the development of the national culture with a sense of originality, needless to say, that students be educated in such a manner as to cultivate their full understanding of the spirit and achievements of their forefathers. This will lead them to endeavor to develop their cultural heritage so as to preserve it for posterity.

Among Korea's folk dances, the farmers dance is considered most ideal for utilization in formal education. My research is, therefore, designed to find means of further propagating it for ultimate adoption in school curricula. However, the writer, in the process of the research, was confronted with a paucity of historical material and literature on the basis of which to trace the development of this dance. Although a few research reports and publications in this field are available, most of them do not go beyond the introduction of Korean folk customs and so they are insufficient in terms of probing into the detailed aspects of the farmers dance.

Especially research has never been conducted into, and no records are available concerning, the technical aspects of the dance. Regretfully, this study drew the conclusion that the musical patterns and performing skills of the dance unique to localities are gradually disappearing. It is, therefore, very important that extensive research be organized as soon as possible so that these traditions can be recorded and thus preserved before they face extinction.

The writer is convinced from his research that the farmers dance, which developed on the basis of the activity in farming, is a "sound dance" and, being full of momentum, is considered to be very effective in building up the physical strength of students and enriching their emotional life. My research could not be concluded in a short period of time. Much money was required in order to visit many localities to make up for the lack of literature concerning local differences in the farmers dance.

This research work, therefore, is divided into the first and second phases, the former consisting of a general examination of and a study into the methods of applying it to formal education while the latter is devoted to the collection of scores by means of local field surveys and a comparative study into the performing skills found in different localities.

The first phase of the research, which covered the period from March 1, 1965 to March 30, 1967, was based on the theme: "Research into the Farmers Music and Dance, Part I — For Application to Education." Research in this phase included such departments as the development of the farmers music and dance, performing skills, basic movements, the *sogo* (small drum) Dance, reference materials, and other matters related to the farmers music and dance. The following methods were utilized in the research: Acquisition of works of reference, collection of scores, examination of movements of dancers and of their performances, and the drawing up of lessons on the farmers dance for students as an experimental step.

The second phase of the research, which started on April 7, 1967 and will last until March 30, 1969, is devoted to the theme: "Research into the Farmers Music and Dance, Part II — For Comparative Examination of Local Differences." The research will consist of the collection of literature and reference materials, recording of music and collection of scores from different localities throughout the country, comparative examination of rhythm patterns and performing skills which are different according to locality, and the publication or announcement of research results. The second phase will also include field surveys.

Historical Development

Origin — Although no historical records authentically document the origin and development of the farmers music and dance, it is generally believed that its origin can be traced back to ancient times when Korean tribesmen established settlements and started farming. This supposition is based on the fact that the movements of the dance are similar to farming actions and that the farmers dance has existed as an attachment to a *dure*, a collective labor unit, a peculiar aspect of Korea's rural life.

The oldest work recording Korean rural life is Chen Shou's (陳壽) *Sam Kuo Chih* (三國誌) which the Chinese historian wrote in 297 A.D. after a visit to Korea. He states: "In Mahan the people held a festival to honor God at the time of sowing in May and of harvesting in October. All of them assembled together, enjoyed singing and dancing day and night without pause, forming lines, circling around, stamping on the ground and clapping their hands according to set rhythms." This description indicates that the ancient dance differed little from the present-day farmers dance in which scores of farmers circle around in lines, tramp on the ground, bend and stretch to the accompaniment of music.

It is evident that Korea's farmers music and dance was developed before the dawn of the Three Kingdoms period. As the nation's unique dance has close connection with its agricultural system, it will help to gain a full understanding of it to examine agricultural activities in Korea.

Dure — A system of collective labor which has been widely practised in Korean agriculture since ancient times. The *dure* is a nationwide labor organization in farming communities that has been not only necessary for collective farming but also for unity of rural communities. Each *dure* had its farmers music and dance band and such bands lent variety to any otherwise routine rural existence.

Discipline was strictly observed in collective farming. Usually a long bamboo pole bearing a standard with the inscription "Farmers Are the Principals of the World" led a group of farmers to their day's work. A farmers' band played throughout the work day. The farmers would normally take rest three or four periods during the day.

From the above it can be concluded that farmers music was developed as a means of helping farmers promote their efficiency by easing the fatigue of a hard day, elevating the ability of the *dure*, and cultivating the spirit of cooperation and the idea of collective responsibility for the ultimate purpose of solidifying unity in a community.

By playing music, farmers were able to unite socially, double their efficiency, and discharge, in a rather jovial mood, an arduous work they could hardly have fulfilled had it not been for music. Thus their hoes could till the soil deeper.

Although farmers music developed with the purpose of stimulating farm work, it gradually became the traditional rural pastime as it was handed down from generation to generation, providing the people with the opportunity to pray for peace and for the longevity and well-being of their co-workers. In addition, music was utilized for rituals to honor the heaven and enhance morale in times of hardship and national upheaval.

Such a system of collective labor was used not only in farming but also for such cottage industries as spinning and weaving by the womenfolk. The most outstanding characteristic of the *dure* was the fact that labor, farmers music and dance, and meals were participated in by all members.

Led by a standard with the inscription *Farmers Are the Principals of the World,* dancers are ready to perform their skills.

Influence of *Nam-sadang*

The farmers music and dance, which grew purely out of farming activities, was soon influenced by the *nam-sadang* in the middle of the Koryŏ dynasty era (about 1300 A.D). It will be helpful to know what the *sadang* were.

The *sadang* can be compared to the gypsies of Central Europe. They roamed the country earning a livelihood by singing and dancing and acrobatic feats. At times the *yŏ-sadang* (female *sadang*) practised prostitution and the *nam-sadang* (male *sadang*) went in for sodomy. Due to the social evils they gave rise to through arson and licentiousness they were finally governed by government regulations and so they fled to the refuge of rural villages.

The acrobatic dances practised by *nam-sadang* find their origin in the Tartars of northern Manchuria and Central Asia. As the *sadang* resettled in Korea as farmers after wandering the country, their acrobatic feats came to be absorbed into the Korean farmers dance making the latter more colorful. The *Mudong-ch'um*, Twirling of the *sangmo*, and Spinning a Plate on a Stick are examples.

In the *Mudong-ch'um*, four or five men form a pyramid one standing on the shoulders of the other. A boy dressed as a girl stood atop. As the men dance the boy moves his arms and shoulders gracefully.

The *sangmo* dancer wears a long paper streamer suspended from a swivel atop his hat. By rotating his head the long streamer twirls around in circles.

The third feat consisted of a plate placed on the tip of a long bamboo smoking pipe or pole and twirled around by manipulating the hand.

It is also evident that the pure, original farmers dance and music was subject to Mongolian influences to a considerable degree through the *nam-sadang* in view of the fact that the Korean people adopted Mongolian customs in hairdress and clothing during the Koryŏ period, that Northeast Asian hobbies and the various acrobatic feats of Yüan were in vogue in Koryŏ times and that even now practitioners of the farmers dance wear belts and use the *sangmo* that are foreign to Korea.

Frequent folk-dance contests held since the liberation in 1945 provided troupes from various localities with an opportunity to intermingle and this, in turn, has resulted in the disappearance of local features. At present a repertoire usually includes the twirling of the *samgmo* and the *Mudong-ch'um*. Though colorful, the present form of the dance cannot be considered unique to Korea.

Composition of a Troupe

Although there are few differences according to locality, the normal small farmers dance troupe has a *soe* or *kkwoenggari* (small gong), a *changgo* (two-headed, lashed drum), and a *jing* (large gong) assisted by a *puk* (drum) and a *sogo* (small drum).

A larger group, made up of dancers from several villages, has a larger number of instruments, including, besides those enumerated above, the *hojŏk* (horn) and even the *chegŭm* (violin) in some localities.

A farmers band is led by two standard-bearers, one carrying the flag of his troupe and the other an elongated standard suspended from a tall bamboo pole carrying the inscription "Farmers Are the Principals of the World." They are followed by a *mudong* (dancing boy) and a hunter. The Kyŏnggi Provincial troupe, which is representative of the larger bands, consists of two bearers of the farmers flag, two bearers of the troupe flag, three *kkwoenggari*, two *jing*, four *changgo*, two *puk*, eight *sogo*, one *hojŏk* players, and two *mudong* performers.

Instruments

Kkwoenggari — This instrument is made of iron and measures 25 centimeters in diameter. It takes the lead in farmers music, producing rhythm and exchanging dialogue with the drums. Held in the left hand, it is struck with a wooden mallet held in the right hand to produce a metallic sound.

Jing — This instrument is similar in shape to the *kkwoenggari* but much larger. Made of iron, it measures 40 centimeters in diameter. It is struck usually at the starting rhythm of each sub-stanza with a sound that trails and is full of suggestions. It performs a pivotal role by controlling the tempo in the farmers dance. In use in China since ancient times, it was sometimes used to sound warnings or call people together. Held in the left hand, it is struck with a wooden stick having a nob of straw or cloth at its extreme. It was introduced to Korea from China in 1352 A.D., during the reign of King Kongmin of Koryŏ.

Changgo — In ancient times this instrument was made of baked tiles but now it is made of paulownia. It is shaped like a large hourglass measuring one meter in length, and its middle is lashed. Its two heads are made of dog, ox, or horse skin stretched tightly over an iron plate. Like *kkwoenggari*, it has a lead role but it is more delicate, graceful and flexible than the former in terms of indicating rhythm changes. The size of the *changgo* differs according to its usage. The one used for

Musical Instruments for Farmers Dance

Left photo: *Jing* (left), measuring 40 centimeters in diameter, is similar in shape to *Kkwoenggari* (right) but much larger.
Right photo: *Hojōk,* made of iron, produces so high volume that its sound can compete with the combined volume of all the other instruments.

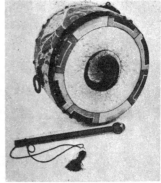

Changgo is shaped like a large hourglass measuring one meter in length and its middle is lashed. Its two heads are covered with animal skin.

Puk, measuring 35 meters in diameter, is similar in shape to the Western drum. It is covered with animal skin on both sides.

farmers music can be hung over the shoulder and is struck with a cloth-tipped wooden stick held in the right hand and with a bamboo stick held in the left hand.

Puk—Measuring 30 centimeters in diameter, this instrument, like the *changgo*, is covered with skin and hollow inside. It usually signifies a strong rhythm or is struck at each rhythm. Its sound is simple but its volume is so large as to be heard at a distance. A primitive instrument, it is carried over the left shoulder and struck with a wooden mallet held in the right hand.

Sogo—Measuring 15 centimeters in diameter, this instrument is made of wood and has a handle. The body is hollowed and both sides are covered with dog skin. The sound it produces is small and simple and thus it has no significant musical function. But it is indispensable to the dance as the only indicator of dance rhythms. Held in the left hand by its handle, it is struck with the right hand while being brandished right and left, forward and backward. It is mostly used to beat the dancing rhythms after the farmers have quaffed a bowl or two of rice wine at the end of a day's work rather than during working hours.

Hojŏk—One meter in length, this instrument is made of iron and can be separated into two parts so as to be more easily carried. With a high-pitched sound, it is often used for signaling purposes. Most melodic among the farmers musical instruments, the *hojŏk* is so rich in volume that its sound alone can compete with the combined volume of all the other instruments. It is blown when the same melody is repeated or on an impromptu basis. This instrument was introduced to Korea from Central Asia by way of China in 1352.

Time of Performance

Generally speaking, the famers music and dance is performed on the following occasions:

1. January 15th by the lunar calendar to celebrate the beginning of a new year. This performance is dedicated to praying for prosperity and a rich harvest.

2. At the time of transplanting the rice seedlings, in May by the lunar calendar. As this is a busy season for farmers, the performances are designed to promote the efficiency of those laboring.

3. At the time of weeding in June by the lunar calendar. Also for the promotion of work efficiency.

4. Farmers Day (July 15 by the lunar calendar). Farmers, now that the weeding is completed, can relax for a while.

5. On the day of the Moon Festival (August 15 by the lunar calendar). This also is an auspicious day for farmers.

6. At the time of harvest in October by the lunar calendar. Farmers celebrate the completion of another year's farming with music and dance.

As the above list shows, the farmers dance is performed on important rural occasions and thus has close ties with agriculture. These occasions also correspond to Korea's traditional holidays or festivals. Hence, it is apparent that the farmers music and dance are important aspects of national recreation.

Contents of Performance

The contents of a performance, generally speaking, consist of about 10 items. There are a few differences according to locality.

Performance variations include those: centered on changes in ranks as in the Western square dance, mixed with dramatic flavor, dedicated more to music, dedicated more to dance, most of which are a recent production; based on farming activities with such sequences as plowing, stepping across seedling beds, transplanting rice seedlings, sharpening sickles, harvesting rice, husking rice, and making straw rope and straw bags; and dances with martial and religious themes. Performances also include group and individual renditions to produce colorful effects.

Group performances — Especially in a larger troupe there are many varieties in formation. Examples are the circle formation, the line formation and the square formation.

The circle formation includes a single circle, a double circle, an S-shaped circle, a volute circle, five volute circles, an 8-shaped circle; four circles, each surrounded by a larger one, formed by 16 dancers who, divided into four groups to embody the cross, run in the same direction; and four circles formed by 16 dancers who, also divided into four groups in the shape of a cross, run in the direction which alternates with their neighboring group.

The line formation consists of a single line and double lines facing each other.

The square formation takes two forms, one places four dancers in line in the four corners and the other is formed by 16 dancers standing in four lines.

Individual performances — As the dancers stand in two lines facing each other, one of their number appears in his turn and performs the feat of twirling a long streamer around his head

Dancers show the feat of twirling their streamers to the accompaniment of *changgo.*

while playing the *sogo*. Another individual feat is done by the *sangsoe*, the troupe leader, who, while playing the *kkwoenggari*, also twirls a streamer around his head. The 12-fathom streamer twirling is another. A streamer attached to the hat of a dancer measures 12 fathoms in length. But it is not true that the longer his streamer, the better his technique. It is recommended that the length of a streamer corresponds to the height of its wearer. In any case, various fascinating skills are shown in the twirling of a streamer.

The *jing* player also presents various fine performances while playing his instrument. The instrument is hard to play even though it looks very simple. The *Mudong-ch'um* is rendered by a boy dancer dressed in a girl's costume who stands atop dancers who form a pyramid of two, three, four, or even five stories.

The playing of the two *changgo* heralds a glorious finale to the farmers dance. They are played in various rhythms.

This research, as stated above, was conducted for the purpose of finding means of utilizing the farmers music and dance in education. Many unexpected difficulties confronted the researcher, mainly the lack of reference materials. This report is intended to systematize whatever knowledge is obtained from the research project and to adjust it as extensively as possible. It is to be regretted that this report does not include an elaborate explanation of the basic steps in the farmers dance and the playing of the *sogo* which provides the lead rhythms, examples of performances, designs of the musical instruments used in the dance, and the costumes. These matters will be dealt with on a later occasion.

Two more years are needed to complete this research project. The second phase will be devoted to an analysis of local differences in costumes, performance methods, and movements. Much money is required to conduct the second phase because it involves field surveys to film the dance and record the sound.

As explained above, the farmers music and dance has been part of Korea's rural life for many centuries and it has developed as a sound art form. It includes all the steps and movements required by the Western folk dance, is creative, it requires body movements from head to foot, and enables dancers to display individual expression. For this reason the farmers music and dance is believed ideal for application to formal education. However, its educational value is not limited to physical culture. It can also promote understanding of Korea's unique emotional life.

This writer is making efforts to modernize the basic steps of the dance so as to facilitate its popularization. Many years of continued study and adjustment are needed, however, before any results will be seen.

Society of Korean Dance Studies Debuts in West Germany, New York, Honolulu

ALAN C. HEYMAN

The Society of Korean Dance Studies, founded in 1981 under the leadership of Prof. Kim Mae-ja of the Dance Dept. of Ewha Womans University in Seoul, made their first foreign appearance beginning in West Germany on July 6th, 1982, under the auspices of the German Institute for Korean Studies. Following a series of performances in Berlin, Hamburg and Frankfurt, the members of the Society journeyed to New York, where they participated in the "East Meets West in Dance" workshop at New York University from July 12-17, sponsored by the Dept. of Dance & Dance Education. The workshop climaxed on the night of July 16th with a dance performance given by the members of the Society. The travelling performance series was brought to a close with a presentation at the InterArts Hawaii Festival on July 27th.

On the opening day of the workshop at New York University, the members of the Society saw a videotape presentation of the modern dance entitled "Chinook" (meaning "Warm Breeze" or "Spring Breeze") composed by Laura Brittain, professor of dance at New York University. They then learned excerpts from the work and discussed with the composer herself the symbolization used. The evening was devoted to a viewing of the videotape entitled "Aesthetics of East and West," based on the works of Georgia O'Keefe, a visual artist, as discussed by F.S.C. Northrup.

On the second day, Pearl Lang, a disciple of the renowned modern dancer, Martha Graham, conducted a class on "Beyond Graham-based technique," which was followed by a live presentation of a repertory work from Korea, conducted by Prof. Kim Mae-ja and performed by the members of the society.

For her presentation, Prof. Kim chose a work she had composed entitled "Dance and *Sinmyŏng*." Prior to the presentation, Prof. Kim made the following introductory remarks in regard to the work itself:

> The performance which will be presented today, entitled "Dance and *Sinmyŏng*," was premiered this year in Seoul, Korea, to mark the first anniversary of the founding of the Society of Korean Dance Studies.
>
> This composition, which is based on a traditional form of dance that was performed out-of-doors, employs the rhythm of Korean traditional percussion instruments and is based on movements taken, in general, from Korean traditional mask dance-drama, farmer's festival music and dance, and other various types of folk dance movements. The basic form, however, is taken from farmer's festival music and dance.
>
> Our traditional dance, from very remote ancient times, has been continuously developed and passed on down from generation to generation. From the time of the Yi dynasty (1392-1910), of all group performances, it may be deduced today that the mask dance-drama, in particular, was the most actively developed.
>
> In light of this fact, we then have to ask ourselves today why our national dance tradition has fallen into the present state of stagnation. An awareness of the gravity of this problem and how to deal with it systematically has come about only recently.
>
> Though the succession of tradition as an affirmative concept, the audience's aesthetic artistic experience, a collective awareness of society as a whole, and other factors must be duly considered; at the same time the fact that we are compelled to look at our dance with a new vision must also be

stressed. This rests entirely on the efforts we exert in creating our new dance compositions.

This composition, "Dance and *Sinmyŏng*," in comparison with the simplistic dances in existence today, challenges us with the three following questions:

Why do we dance?
What is dance to me?
How can I unify my life with my dance?

Keeping these questions in mind, we can thus arrive at the understanding that the audience shares the same artistic experience as the dancers themselves and strives to materialize this personal artistic experience into everyday life itself.

The opening part of this composition is associated with the "Road Play" that is found in farmer's festival music and dance, and also in the mask dance-drama, in which all the participants enter the performing area in single file, playing musical instruments and dancing in time with the music. The "Road Play" traditionally represents the opening part of the performance, as it also does here. The latter part of this composition is based on a dance taken from a type of folk exorcistical ritual called *twi-p'uri*. It is characterized by both slow and fast dance movement patterns that continue throughout the piece, performed to the accompaniment of the percussion instrumental ensemble.

Sinmyŏng, which literally translated, means "God's Order" or "God's Command," but actually has a much wider, all-encompassing connotation, is actively created with the backing of an aesthetic consciousness, which is a kind of inclination of joy. This inclination, in turn, is the very fountainhead of the living folk art of the people. It can only be experienced when we can dismantle and thus free ourselves from such things as suppression, suffering and pain, hate, the sorrow of parting, and, yes, even death itself, by transforming tragedy into comedy. We can also win freedom from that which is difficult by experiencing that which is joyful through a combination of an aesthetic artistic experience and *Sinmyŏng*.

In this composition, the first part is executed in total darkness. In the scene that follows, the process of *Sinmyŏng* is evoked in joyful dance movements. Inspired by the rhythms of the percussion ensemble, the performers struggle with and fight forcibly against pain. Though suppression and pain continue, they fight on still more adamantly to break these forces that dwell within them. In addition, they sing a folk song, together with the percussion ensemble, that embodies an expression of pain. This three-dimensional force of music, dance and song spurs them to even greater inspiration to overpower the sickness that besieges them. At last, the performers' vigor to fight on is given sustenance by the aesthetic artistic experience they are able to draw upon from *Sinmyōng*. It is then that the dance movements of the performers and that of the equally inspired audience — who share deeply the same aesthetic experience — is no longer discernable; and, it is then that the folk ritual of exorcism (*twip'uri*) is spontaneously created and comes into being of itself.

The above-mentioned is a process in which an art is typified. We can feel more a sense of reality in this art since its mode of processing was obtained from our very own historical experience. Also, the typical patterns developed through this process each bear their own style of performance in accordance with each era's historical background. Moreover, the differing styles of performance have each added a new vitality and elegance to the dance, and that is why a specific art's historical and social background is of such great importance.

This composition, "Dance and *Sinmyōng*," offers us the opportunity to re-examine the reality of Korean dance today; that is, modern dance must reflect modern reality. If this composition supplies reality to examine modern dance and enables us to experience a vital artistic *Sinmyōng* by sharing the artistic experience with the audience, then an unfading ethical utopia will not only exist in a world of dreams, but, through vital *Sinmyōng*, it will become a very real part of our everyday existence.

Following this, Ernestine Stodelle, a disciple of the renowned modern dancer Doris Humphrey, conducted a performance and theoretical discussion of "Ecstatic Themes" of Doris Humphrey. In the evening, this author chaired a discussion on "Sources of Aesthetic Content of Korean and Far Eastern Dance."

The following day, Philip Merrifield, Professor of Psychology at New York University, led a discussion of "Arts and Humanities — Symbolic Languages of East and West," which was followed by a lecture-demonstration presented by both the author and Prof. Kim, Mae-ja on the various dance movement patterns found in Korean court, folk and ritual dance.

On Thursday, July 15th, Prof. Laura Brittain once again took the podium and gave a lecture-demonstration on Western dance improvisation entitled "Eastern Content as an Inspiration for Western Dance in its Primary Function."

The following day, the presentation was once again made by the author together with Prof. Kim Mae-ja under the heading "The Aesthetic of Traditional Korean Dance," at which time Prof. Kim read a paper entitled "The Spirit and Soul of Korean Dance," the content of which follows:

> Korean dance is a type of dance which has a deep, profound spiritual background, and which has as its basis oriental religion and philosophy. In addition, it is also a dance which evolved into a form that became endowed with elegance and refinement, but which, at the same time, was imbued with a sense of the state of nothingness, whose rhythm was that which sprang forth from nature itself and was conveyed through dance and music, which, in turn, were never thought of as two separate entities, but always as one and inseparable.
>
> When the people of Korea sang and danced and were entertained, their feelings of resentment (specifically, the resentment of females toward the male-dominated Confucian society of the Yi dynasty) passed away. The feelings of resentment that appeared in the dance were a reflection of that which was vividly found in the society itself; but, prior to and after its appearance, resentment was transposed into laughter or gaiety, and calm or composure. This is the process in which the feeling of resentment was conquered or overcome in the process of formation of the Korean artistic system.

Korean dance and music cannot be thought of as being divided from nature and the seasons. Not just from order itself, but from nature's order one finds a beauty that is indeed a treasure of the mind.

From ancient times, on a very fertile land, the harvest was plentiful, the atmosphere always filled with a frequent abundance of the sounds of people exchanging happinesses, and through these people there arose a forest of culture that became the personality of a nation. To go anywhere on the Korean peninsula, to find beautiful songs and dances, was found to have been written in the history books of China, and, after that, during the emergence of the Three Kingdoms period of Silla, Paekche, and Koguryō (37 B.C.–918 A.D.) to the indigenous ancient Shamanism and totemism was added Buddhist-Confucian thought, and thereby many modifications were brought about. There is no doubt that the kings and courtiers of the Three Kingdoms period were very deeply involved with the continental dance of Asia; however, they did not just merely enjoy it, but added a decorative and artistic design which was highly individualistic. Not only in the silk finery of the royal court dances, but extending even to the rough, grass roots dance of the commoners, the influence of the Asian continental civilization changed the Korean culture, and that change resulted in an expression of freedom, showing anything they wanted to show, and showing themselves without hiding anything. It can be understood then that the Koreans did not place emphasis on beauty of the outer form alone, but more so on personality and individuality. This can be illustrated by examining ancient music and dance scores in chronological order. When we do so, we can find many changes and modifications, thus indicating that the Koreans added their own nationalistic personality, or own personal touch, so to say, to that which was brought from the Asian continent.

Overall then, even though at times it may appear to be different, the purpose and target of Korean dance consistently stresses freedom and strong national individuality. That is to say, even though various types of progressive and developmental aspects from foreign countries have been adopted and assimilated, Koreans have always added their own special characteristics to them, and from this admixture have, over a period of time, re-created new forms and developed them into a sublimation of delicacy and fineness.

In ancient times, various rituals were held, such as the "Ritual of Heaven," the "Ritual for Various Spirits," among which the "Ritual for the God of the House" and the "Ritual for the Mountain Spirit" were included. It was from these various rituals that the Korean people attained a strong attachment to the land and also an excessive attachment to the family clan system, the protection of which was supplicated to in many rituals. Also, in the spiritual belief of all the countries that make up East Asia, the concept of heaven ruled over by only one supreme god exists. This being so, even the supreme sovereigns referred to their country as "that which is below Heaven." Together with this concept, though the Koreans' way of thought lay in a deep attachment to the land, when they gazed upward toward Heaven from their long politically-oriented society, every type of art, without exception, sprang forth. And so it was, too, that this provided the spiritual foundation from which traditional dance grew. The mask dance-dramas, filled with a deep sense of mystery, which have their roots in folk ritual dance, Buddhist ritual dances, which profess the redemption of mankind, added to this the dances of irrepressible joy, almost reaching the point of giddiness, a joy pouring forth from within, from a deep sense of beauty, a state of everlasting exhilaration. These characterize the dances of the itinerant folk troubadours and female entertainers, even reaching to the profound, elegant and extremely graceful royal court dances of the Yi dynasty and those which came before it — all of these dances have their roots in a solid ground which was made firm, after which, step by step, they took wing and flew to the sky and above, toward Heaven.

In conformance with its original beauty, the underlying theory of Korean dance begins from the moment the elegant foot, encased in the width of the *pŏsŏn* (the Korean traditional style bootee that covers the foot), takes its first step. At this moment, the feeling is not one of a human searching the bare ground aimlessly for something, but rather that of a crane or

)

snowy white heron taking wing toward a lofty sky; and, in the case where the dancer is a female, that of a foot hidden beneath the folds of a wide skirt (the so-called Korean traditional *ch'ima* skirt). This is not to be regarded as a situation where the foot is adhering closely to the ground, but rather that of a form in which the foot is avoiding the heavens, a foot which is like a bird in hiding, assimilating both freedom and adherence and consolidating them both into one at the same time. In this manner, Korean dance appears to be lightly dependent on the ground; but, at the same time, there overflows a lightness of beauty that yet retains gravity. Thereby, the special characteristic of Korean dance lies in its complete freedom of expression and movement; also, at the same time, it provides a release from all feelings of guilt or wrongdoing.

These days, in the field of modern dance, there is a lot of discussion about such things as tension and release, considered from an aesthetic viewpoint. However, our predecessors, our forefathers, had already taken all that into consideration, as is evident when we observe the traditional dance. Also, Korean dance is thought of as being only that which is executed with a calm, quiet and passive composure; on the other hand, however, history proves this to be quite different. That is to say, when examining the past history of Korean dances, we find them to be quite magnanimous and extensively magnified at the same time. In addition, though the above-mentioned passiveness is executed in a pattern of "movement in quiet" and "quiet in movement," at the same time it is a calm and quiet that is executed with an infinite amount of energy so as to induce the utmost appeal to the observing audience. Many new dances that are performed today, however, are coquettish, artificial creations that emanate from a very superficial feeling that is quite unmindful of the original nature of Korean dance. Korean dance was imbued and nurtured with a powerful sense of nature and divine providence, and it is only in this direction that Korean dance should continue to move and be created.

In ancient times, in rites to heavenly deities that were held before the outset of farmwork, such as the new year ritual festivities, when a bumper crop was supplicated for, and after the agricultural cycle was completed, such as the harvest moon festival in the autumn when the farmers gave thanks to the deities for granting them a good harvest, labor and the arts enjoyed a common origin and existed together in harmony and accord. Although, at the time, this phenomenon existed the world over, particularly in Korean culture it was continuously handed down and further propagated among succeeding generations so that it came to form the very basic characteristic of Korean culture. And so it is that among Korean dances, those found in folk rites, folk plays and games, and in folk drama (such as the mask dance-drama) are not separate entities in themselves, but are considered part of an integral whole along with ritual music and drama, a type of *gesamkunstwerk*, so to speak, each having inseparable links with one another.

The role of the dance is to gather together human activities which are scattered and divided. It can also be said that the dance is a manifestation of the core linking all types of human activities and, at the same time, represents the quintessence of Korean culture.

In a general sense, the dance in Korea may be divided into two categories: that which is danced by the average person as part of his everyday life and work when he is so moved by interest and divine inspiration, and that which is danced by a professional who learns the dance through discipline, experience, and his own inherent gifts or natural talent.

How art can be integrated into everyday life through a feeling of deep interest and divine inspiration is hereby contemplated.

When we acknowledge the fact that every person can actually participate in artistic activities because art is attained in life by experience through which it matures of its own accord, we can strongly and affirmatively advocate the position of folk art — the significance and impact of growth emanating from the common people being the essence of folk art.

Recognizing the fact that the dance undergoes large-scale changes as it is handed down throughout the generations, and examining some of these changes, we should first consider the prehistoric and succeeding Tribal States period of Korea, which began some three or four-thousand years ago and continued up until around the year 57 B.C. At that time, life and existence was highly geared to the matter of expediency, and so the dances of that period were largely dedicated to various gods in the belief that such warded off adversity, and further that, in the society itself, no distinction was made between the aristocracy and the common people. However, in the succeeding Three Kingdoms period, the upper classes took it upon themselves of their own accord to perform songs and dances, and out of this deep concern for music and dance, songs and dances developed appropriately in due course. A good example of this is the *hwarang*, an organization of young men comparable to the knights of medieval Europe, who sought out mountains and streams where they delighted in the performance of an art that was both elegant, erudite and, at the same time, aesthetically pleasing. As time passed these young men amassed a wealth of discipline and technique in the execution of their art, and also at the height of the Buddhist period when the high priests acquired the knowledge of music and dance and brought it up to a high degree of excellence.

In this process then, dance first functioned as a part of work and everyday life of the common people. Later, with the emergence of an upper strata culture, training of body and spirit, as well as religious and ideological expression, were sought through the medium of the dance. Still later, during the Yi dynasty, under the code of Confucian ethics, the performance of dance as a profession was relegated to the entertainer class, one of the designated lower castes, while the aristocracy and literati were restricted from taking any part in such, except for occasional self-enjoyment purely in an amateur-dilettantish type of situation, and were thereby allowed only to take part as spectators, or those for whom the entertainment was specifically provided. And so, in the early part of the Yi dynasty, the distinction between performer and spectator was clearly defined; however, in the latter part, the schism once again narrowed, and one and all sectors of the society took part in group dance performances together irregardless of social status, as had been done previously.

Of all dances, the royal court dance is perhaps that which is most highly regarded in terms of taste and refinement, having been looked upon by audiences in general as that which was the very essence of Korean culture. Yet, paradoxically, though the art itself was held in the very highest esteem, the performers themselves were still looked down upon as lower strata society, and the restrictions thereby imposed upon them as such inhibited their freedom of expression as performing artists.

In the latter part of the Yi dynasty, however, a new movement arose in folk art whereby, once again, class distinctions were overcome and people from the upper strata culture were gradually drawn to the folk art of the common people.

After the fall of the Yi dynasty and the emergence of the modern period, all arts, the dance in particular, underwent a dramatic change and rapidly developed to a stage whereby they rose far above the heads of the common people, so that once again a large gap emerged between the artist and audience. This time, however, it was not one of class distinction, as had been the case previously, but rather due to the aspirations of the performers themselves, who continually sought to attain a higher level art form, and, in so doing, appealed to an ever-diminishing audience of art connoisseurs and afficionados, so to speak, thereby losing popular support. This is not to say that folk art was forgotten entirely, but that in the performer's quest for a more sophisticated art form, such phenomena as group folk dance, in which the audience, at one time played an active role, was sorely neglected.

Why then, we must ask ourselves, did this tendency come about? The answer lies in the fact that our long traditional culture was interrupted, first by the Japanese colonial annexation in 1910, which brought about an end to the Yi dynasty, and later by the devastating Korean War of 1950. As a result, for the average person leisure time to contemplate and enjoy the arts was virtually non-existent, since he was solely occupied with the question of survival itself, not to mention other factors involved. Due to this weak point in the cultural life of the people, the onslaught of Western culture from the turn of the century onward practically drove the traditional arts into extinction, and thereby many superficial dance forms without traditional roots emerged on the scene.

And so we of the contemporary Korean dance world have once again turned about to find these roots, a search in which we are now actively engaged. And, in our quest for such, our choreography must modernize and develop the dance, not only in just scratching the surface of the modern and traditional, of East and West, not only in form and content, but with a strong concept and recognition of our nation's cultural legacy and historical tradition. It is with this concept that we must look toward new directions in the creation and composition of our dances in the future to come.

That evening, at the Murray Bergtraum High School Theatre in New York, the Society of Korean Dance Studies presented a program of both traditional dances and new dances composed by Prof. Kim, based on traditional dance movements and themes.

The program began with a royal court dance of Chinese origin entitled *Hŏnsŏndo* ("Peaches Consecrated to Mountain Fairies") in which a table set with large peaches was set at center front stage and offered to the monarch in both dance and song. The peaches derive from a Taoist legend which states that whosoever tasted the peaches would be blessed with long life. This dance dates from the Koryŏ period (935-1392 A.D.), and belongs to the *Tangak* classification, which signifies that it originated in either Tang or Sung dynasty China. Though the choreography is based on the dance as it is recorded in such ancient chronicles as the *Akhakkwebŏm* ("Cardinal Principles of Music") and the *Chŏngjae holgi*, an ancient work on court dance, the dance was slightly modified so that it could be adopted to the modern stage.

The above was followed by the "*Sanjo*," a folk instrumental improvisatory piece which was set to a solo dance created and

Prof. Kim Mae-ja dances in a solo capacity in the *Sanjo*, which is accompanied by improvisatory instrumental music.

performed by Prof. Kim Mae-ja. Another one of her more modern compositions followed, "The Pulley," whose meaning is best conveyed by a poem she composed to accompany the dance:

> Though by mother's teeth
> Your umbilical cord was cut,
>
> In reality,
> It is a cord
>
> That can never
> Be broken.
>
> Though I be buried,
> Though you and I be buried,
>
> Though the placenta,
> It, too, be buried,
>
> We return.
>
> Never ending,
> Doth return, and

Without end,
Doth the spring breeze blow.

"The Pulley" reveals a certain stage of freedom by accepting bondage; in this work, meeting and parting, life and death are bound by a string of fate, then loosened, then turned into bondage. This concept is transmitted through the music and dance, in which neither takes preference over the other, and in which, as a result, there is discord in harmony, and, at the same time, harmony indiscord. Freedom amid bondage clearly points out, then, that the deep-rooted *chŏnghan* (resentment) of Korean women is not merely tears, the acceptance of the bondage of transmigration is not mere resignation, and what may appear outwardly as quiet beauty, elegant simplicity and profoundness is actually a cloak of powerful inner emotion: they are not following the way of Taoism and Confucianism blindly. This very moving theme awakens one to the Korean disposition, which, with intensity hidden, can inspire one to sacrifice himself without hesitation in the face of adversity.

A solo performance of the folk version of the "Buddhist Monk Dance," performed by Kim Jong-nyuh, followed, and another composition by Prof. Kim Mae-ja, entitled "Quadrason," brought the first part of the program to a close.

In "Quadrason," four musical instruments native to Korea—the large and small gong, round and hourglass-shaped drum—represent a universe comprised of the sun, moon, stars and man. The dance exhibits the beauty of harmonious living in the universe with the introduction of traditional Oriental morality into the dance movements (respect for parents and the aged, conjugal love, dedication to the upbringing of children, and good Samaritanism). The cosmological and Korean traditional morality and reality that the four instruments possess are valued over the comforts of modern civilization.

Here again, the essence of the composition is most aptly

expressed in the following poem, composed by Prof. Kim:

In the beginning,
When this world was created,

Sky and earth
Were one.

No plant nor beast
Did there exist.

In one sound, and
In one flash of light,

Did the universe appear, and
Did mankind come into being.

Stamp your feet and
Break the ground!

Clap your hands and
Reverberate the sky!

Shout in unison and
Rock the universe!

Standing firmly
On our earth,

With the large and small gong,
With the round and hourglass-shaped drum,

With the sun, moon, stars and man,

Let us make a joyful sound
Unto the sky!

Against the rather feminine and continuous experimental method in "The Pulley," "Quadrason" is an experiment done in a masculine and unconventional method.

The second part of the program opened with still another of Prof. Kim's compositions, "The Potsherds." Pottery has long been in use in Korea. Its fragments, long buried under the ground, appeared on the surface after a rain-fall or during the rainy season. The potsherds were favorite toys for children at a time when there was little else to play with. Pottery fragments were a familiar sights to most Koreans at one time.

In this work, Prof. Kim presents the most realistic and implicit representation of vitality—dead but resurrecting, broken and buried but exposed—thus emphasizing humanism by elevating human pain (war, disease, poverty) to a religious level. It is a synchronizing recreation of modern dance.

Here again, the essence of the dance is captured in poetry:

Sunlight shines on the potsherds
In the sandy field.

How long the day is
For the broken potsherds.

Ah, how cruel the sun is;
Will her relentless rays never cool?

The sandy field has
Burned to white

You are bleeding, potsherds,
The whole day,

Rolling in
The sandy field;

Potsherds one,
Potsherds two,
Potsherds ten,

Both you and I.

A solo instrumental interlude on the *taegŭm* (transverse bamboo flute), played by Kim Yŏng-dong, followed, and this in turn was succeeded by a dance from the *Chinogwi kut*, a folk ritual from the Seoul area held for the safe passage of a departed soul into Paradise. A solo mask dance from the *Pongsan* mask dance-drama, which originated in Hwanghae Province (presently in north Korea) comprised the fourth

A scene from the *Silk Road*

number on the program, and the final presentation was
another of Prof. Kim's compositions entitled "The Silk Road,"
set to music composed by veteran *kayagŭm* (twelve-stringed
instrument) player Hwang Pyŏng-gi.

The main themes of "The Silk Road" are the traditional
docility and immense maternal capacity intrinsic to the
women born on this soil, and the long and wide skirt, called
the *ch'ima*, traditionally worn by Korean women. The vast
ch'ima embraces and beautifies abhorrence, pain and joy. The
movements originate from the folk and Buddhist ritual dance
tradition.

"The Silk Road" is best summed up in yet another of Prof.
Kim's poetic compositions:

Even though we suffered
Endless pain and hardship,

Our culture steadfastly flowered.

It is maintained in our blood,
With patience and courtesy,

Like a ray of light.

Our culture, graced with
Modesty and nobility,

Will flow in our hearts,
On the eternal Silk Road,

Spreading beautifully,
As long as our pulse shall beat.

A Look at the Korean National Ballet

CHRISTINE J. LOKEN

The arts present us with a condensed picture of the cultures from which they spring. The aesthetic values which are presented when different cultures handle the same mediums give us an insight into their people; their physique, physical environment, and social customs. All of the arts do this to a certain degree, each focusing on different aspects of life. Yet dance stands in a unique position, for only through dance can we see the body image of a people. Through studying the basic characteristics of a country or culture's dance; its movement vocabulary and the relationships between dancers, we can gain an insight into often unconscious areas of body identification and learned movement behavior.

This idea was very evident in "Les Sylphids" the June performance of the Korean National Ballet, and acted as a catalyst for the writing of this article.

The problems of transplanting Western arts on Eastern soil, or Eastern arts on Western soil are manifold. Within this century there has been quite a movement in Asia to adopt Western arts along with Western technology. More recently the trend has begun moving in the opposite direction, with Eastern arts coming to the West along with Eastern religions and philosophies.

In some areas this exchange is accomplished with relative ease. The two styles may coexist within the same environment with both operating at a high level of proficiency. In Korea for example, there has been a great interest in Western Classical Music and several Koreans have gained international fame as concert musicians. Dance because of its dependence on the body itself as a means of expression, and its close connection with cultural body image, is not as easy to transplant as an art which has another medium of expression.

It would be very difficult for a Korean to be able to master the intricacies of ballet without being surrounded by people whose basic aesthetic principles were in accord with those of ballet, just as it would probably be impossible for a Westerner to execute Korean dance with a feeling of *mŏt* and *hŭng* without having been totally immersed in Korean life and culture.

As the exchange of arts broadens, it may be useful to look at where we are coming from in order to understand where we are going. In other words, to look at the aesthetic bases of the arts in their own countries so that we can better appreciate the changes that occur in these forms as they begin to grow in their new homes. Some of these forms may be too deeply based on the ancient history of the people, their religious philosophies and language, to make them transplantable to a new time and culture. In this case, an art may be appreciated outside of its place of origin, but always as a novelty; something which is beautiful for its very inscrutableness and not as something which can ever be integrated into the aesthetic whole of the place in which it finds itself presented.

In fact, some arts may be so connected with a specific time in history that they are unable to retain their hold even within their own countries, as shown by the "conscious preservation" status into which many arts have fallen in recent times.

Some Western forms, and modern ballet seems to be one of them, have become so connected with the values of the technological society from which they spring that they seem to have moved into the position of belonging to all technological societies. In recent years, as nations become more highly developed in a technological sense we find an increasing interest in the exploration of ballet as a modern expressive dance form.

Ballet grew out of the European court tradition, but in recent years has taken on qualities which bind it closely to industrial societies. For example: the speed with which movements are executed, the placement of the body; weight slightly forward ready for movement, spine straight, chest thrust forward, the emphasis on covering space, traveling across the stage area, jumping both up and across space to escape gravity, defying the laws of nature rather than flowing with them, and the extreme emphasis on individual virtuosity. This new ballet speaks of people who are striving for power over themselves and their environment, people who live in cities where the pace of life is fast, people whose lives are tense and controlled, people who live where change and mobility are a way of life, where life and actions are not neat and symmetrical, and where the needs of the individual are of great importance. While in most traditional dance forms actions are initiated on the right and then repeated on the left side, in ballet and other modern dance forms the choreographers feel no compulsion to follow this or any other rule. In fact often modern ballets seem to be an almost continuous stream of new unrelated movements. In classical ballet, the women are portrayed as delicate, ethereal creatures; somewhat retiring, shy and demure, while their male partners' only duty is to gently lift and support these delicate ladies and perhaps execute a few jumps and turns. In the modern ballet, both sexes are coming more and more into their own as individuals; moving out of the crowd and showing themselves in all of their strength and individuality. The themes of ballet are secular and in recent years echoing the alienation which also seems to be part of life in a technological society, where the people are removed from activities which relate to their most basic needs.

The problems of importing a foreign dance form (even

ballet, which for the reasons I have indicated, seems to belong more to an age than a specific country) are manifold and extremely subtle. The resistance, even among those who are its main proponents, to certain of its aspects may be at a totally unconscious level. This resistance, or the inability to make certain minute distinctions between old patterns and new techniques may bring about changes which affect the basic nature of the dance form and change it to conform to the body aesthetics of its new home country. Yet the people affecting these changes may be as unaware of making them as the people outside the culture are of the reasons for the changes being made. All they know is that when they go to the theatre to see the dance they are aware of a distinctly foreign element to it. It may please them or it may bore them but it certainly is not the dance which they knew and loved in New York or London.

In bringing ballet to Korea the stress has been placed on the points of similarity between ballet and Korean traditional dance rather than on the points of diversion. This initial phase of growth has the disadvantage of allowing only a limited amount of the total movement vocabulary to be presented. While it is true that there are certain points of contact between Korean dance and ballet the points of dissimilarity are by far in the majority. At a later stage in its development, with a wider movement vocabulary to work from, it may be that ballet in Korea will develop a new and characteristic form, one which represents the Korean culture through subtle manipulations of time and space rather than through the retention of certain body movements which are directly counter to the ballet tradition.

At present the two styles appear to be cancelling each other out in the areas of dynamics and body positioning. Here are some specific observations on traditional Korean dance and ballet as it is being performed in Korea at the present time. The statements about Korean traditional dance are based on the aesthetics of court dance, *Chŏngjae*, since I feel that it is here that the confusion and overlapping occur and it is this style which must be taken into account if we are to understand the modifications which have taken place in the Korean version of ballet.

The basic principle of Korean court dance might be expressed as "heaviness", *mugŏptta*. Whereas the folk forms are involved in the expression of irrepressible joy and exhilaration (a rough translation of *mŏt* and *hŭng*), court dance is performed in a graceful, noble and solemn manner. It is not this manner alone, however, which expresses the quality of heaviness. The basic movement theme is a rolling and continuous walk, as the dancer sinks into the ground and then rises, only to sink down again. This rising and falling is executed in a gentle and natural manner and seems to follow the breathing cycle. The slight tension of the rising movement is followed by relaxation in the downward portion of the cycle. The arms also move in a sequential manner as the energy which was brought into the chest area on inhalation (the rising, tense portion of the cycle) is allowed to flow outward during the period of exhalation (the sinking, relaxed portion of the cycle). This relaxation and dissipation of energy stresses the sinking portion of the movement and accounts for the emphasis on the quality of heaviness in the dance.

Other primary qualities of Korean court dance are the slow tempo, emphasis on achieving beauty through the line of the costume, and emphasis on the curve as the basic element of design. The movements of the arm act to accentuate the curve of the sleeve as the costume and the dancer's movements act together to continually restate the beauty of the curve. The dancer's arms, legs and torso are completely covered and with every movement the costume flows and changes shape around her. The center of weight is held loosely in the upper chest and shoulder area and shifts slightly as the shoulders rise and fall.

In contrast to this, Western ballet stresses height and space, as the dancers strive to extend the bounds of gravity which enslaves them. Quick mercurial steps are often followed by a slight retention of state, so that the dance progresses by stops and starts rather than in the continual rolling fashion of the Korean dance. The dancer maintains a "pulled up" position from the lower abdomen to the sternum and extending on into the lifted position of the chin and head. This constant awareness or tension in the dancer's torso places the center of weight in the pelvis and provides a strong base for the footwork and leg gestures in ballet. The ballet dancer works from a "turned out" position, the legs rotated outward at the hips. This provides a broad base for balance and allows for a greater range of sideward and diagonal movements. Korean dance, in contrast, works from a natural stance neither parallel nor completely turned out but with the heels at an angle of about 30–40°. In ballet the emphasis is on the line, and to that end the arms and legs are often kept as free as possible of excess clothing. Often the arms are bare and the legs covered only by thin tights. Rather than using the movement to accentuate the existing lines in the clothing, the ballet dancer determines the lines in space with his body.

In both Korean dance and classical ballet, the basic position of the arms is an open position in which the arms are extended to the sides from the shoulders. In ballet this is known as second position, while in Korean dance it is *mu*, or dance position. In both of these the arms are kept parallel to the floor, but in ballet the elbows are rotated slightly up and forearms and hands rotated so that the palms of the hands face front, as though holding a large ball. The Korean dance position has the arms and palms facing downward.

These arm positions are an extension of the torso position. In ballet, as mentioned above, the torso is pulled up and lifted. The chest is expanded and the rib cage extended forward so that the spine is straight. In Korean classical dance the upper chest is rounded forward slightly, giving the torso a slightly concave shape. This allows the small jacket of the Korean dress, the *chogŏri*, to lie flat in the front and continue the line of the skirt.

In ballet technique the hand is held in a position with the second finger and thumb brought slightly together. Occasionally the hand will be flicked up or rotated at the end of a movement. Korean classical dance employs a relaxed hand in which fingers and thumb form a single unit in an extension of the line of the arm. Sometimes that line is broken at the wrist in an upward direction as the hand comes down beside the ear, but in general all motions of the hands take place in a downward direction.

In ballet, while the upper portion of the body is often calmly aloof or the arms are moving fluidly from one position to another, the legs are moving with a great deal of articulation. Hip, knee and ankle joints are defined as the leg moves between extended and angular positions. The dancer moves in and out of *plié* (a turned out position with bent knees) as she jumps and turns. In extension the line continues down the leg to the tips of the toes; ankle flexed downward and foot arched to lengthen the line.

In Korean dance the specific line or placement of the leg is of little importance, since it is covered by the costume. Occasionally the foot is lifted so that the toe is seen beneath the edge of the skirt, but the leg does not make extensive gestures. The dancer moves forward by stepping heel first (as in natural walking) and turns also with the weight on the heels. In ballet, the dancer stretches the toe forward in walking, lands on the balls of the feet after a jump, and turns on the toe or ball of the foot.

In the June concert of the National Ballet Co. the blending of Korean and ballet dance styles was evident. Most obvious was the lack of footwork and emphasis on the arm gestures. The traditional Korean influence is also shown in the continuation of the concave line of the torso, only a slight modification having been made in the upper chest. The center of weight has also been retained in the chest area instead of shifting to the pelvis, the mid-torso looking particularly weak without being pulled up and lifted. In view of this it is not surprising that the emphasis remains on the arm gestures. Without the center of weight in the lower torso it is not possible to execute the numerous leg gestures and mercurial steps which make up the ballet technique.

The arm positions themselves have hardly been modified from their Korean positions; the elbows have not been rotated up and back and the hands generally retain their relaxed single unit form. Instead of the continually stretched and expanded arm and chest position of the Western ballet, the arms are carried in a relaxed manner without the alternation of energy and relaxation which is characteristic of the Korean classical dance. Since in the Korean dance the emphasis is on the movement while in the ballet it is on the line of the arm, the Korean dancers are often not attentive to the exact position of their arms and legs. As the arms are held in a relaxed manner, so too the legs do not seem to stretch out endlessly in extensions and jumps. The energy seems to stop just short of the tips of the toes, without the foot curving over in a graceful arch.

Points of divergence between Korean dance and ballet can also be seen in the positioning of the hips and legs. The fully turned out positions of the hips is lacking and prevents the dancers from finding the point of balance they need or being able to lift an extended leg without taking the hip along with it.

Throughout much of the concert, it seemed as though the dancers were dancing in neutral, without either the *mugŏptta* of the classical Korean dance or the speed and height of the ballet technique.

The quality of relaxation is the most difficult aspect of Korean dance for the Westerner to master and his failure to master it is easily seen in the stiff manner in which he performs the *Chŏngjae* or *Talch'um* (masked dance). The continual tension and quality of expansion characteristic of the ballet technique may be equally foreign to the Korean dancer and require a sensitivity to and perception of the problem if he is to master it. All of the observations mentioned above seem to hinge around the aspects of energy and relaxation as they manifest themselves in the two dance forms, classical Korean and ballet.

As mentioned before, this stage of growth may be only an initial one in the growth of ballet in its new home. At this point it seems necessary to evaluate the situation, become aware of its limitations and decide on a course of action for the next stage. In the last section of the June concert, a section uninspiringly entitled "Ballet Concert", the piece "Little Swans" exhibited a surprising amount of footwork. Four dancers, dancing a piece from the ballet "Swan Lake", were quite precise as they executed the little steps and leaps in unison. One could not help wondering why, if they were capable of such lightness and accuracy, they had not been doing it all along. It seems that the directors of the ballet need to ascertain what their aesthetic goals are and decide on a course to attain them. If they wish to present a ballet company here in Korea using the Western classical technique, it appears to be time to call in a guest artist-teacher who can work with the company for a year or two and give them the basic technical skills they require. If they wish to develop their own truly Korean dance form they should take the girls off pointe (without the proper support pointe work can actually be harmful) rename the company and work out a new technique which can make use of the retention of energy and relaxation which is a basic element of Korean dance.

BIBLIOGRAPHY

Heyman, Alan C., *Dances of the Three Thousand-Leagueland*, Seoul: Dong-A, 1966.

Hutchinson, Ahn, *Labanotation, The System of Analyzing and Recording Movement*, New York: Theatre Arts, 1970.

Kealiinohomoku, Joanna, "An Anthropologist Looks at Ballet as a Form of Ethnic Dance" *Impulse*, San Francisco: Impulse Publication, 1970.

Van Zile, Judy, "Energy Use: An Important Stylistic Element in Dance" paper presented at the Joint Conference of the Committee on Research in Dance and the Society for Ethnomusicology, October 1974, San Francisco

History of Korean Theater
1908 – 1945

YI TU-HYŎN

The First Period

The first page of Korea's history of modern theater was written on July 26, 1908 with the opening of the Wŏngak-sa Theater by the novelist-playwright Yi In-jik (1861-1916). However, Korea's first modern theater was built six years before that date, in 1902, as part of the ceremonies marking the 40th anniversary of King Kojong's coronation. This was a small amphitheater with a capacity of 500 to 600 and in which *kisaeng* (entertainment girls), *p'ansori* singers and clowns held stage rehearsals.

Although small, the amphitheater (at whose site the historic Wŏngak-sa Theater, the first modern theater in Korea, was to be opened in later days) was equipped with a stage, with seating for the audience on its three sides, a curtain room and a make-up room.

On the other hand the Ministry of Royal Households in 1902 established an office of stage arts, known as the "Hyŏp-yul-sa," to supervise the *kisaeng* girls and *p'ansori* singers who performed the traditional folk and stage arts for the public. Thus this amphitheater played the role of Korea's first national theater. Unfortunately, the Hyŏp-yul-sa was dissolved in April 1906 due to recriminations made by a Confucian official named Yi Pil-hwa who branded artisans as "erroneous people" from his Confucianistic viewpoint of the stage arts.

The first performance at the Wŏngak-sa Theater, in July 1908, by renowned *kisaeng* and male singers of the capital was more or less in line with the traditional folk art performances presented on the Hyŏp-yul-sa stage.

Modern drama was to wait four more months, until November of that year, when novelist Yi In-jik dramatized his novel *The Silver World* and performed it on the Wŏngak-sa stage on November 15, 1908. In his advertisement in a Seoul daily the author wrote: "In order to improve stage arts in Korea, we are going to present the performance of a novel entitled *The Silver World* two months after the training of the singers begins."

The Silver World, as the author named the dramatized version of his story, became the first "new (modern) drama" performance in Korea. The dramatized novel is presumed to be a play dealing with political enlightenment because the original story was patterned after such Japanese modern dramas as *Soshi-shibai* and *Shosei-shibai.*

Another newspaper advertisement stated that the Wŏngak-sa Theater would present "a new satirical drama entitled *Sugungga* (The Song of the Water Palace) on November 27, 1909. From its title and the contents of the newspaper advertisement, we can deduce that the play was the first attempted dramatization of traditional *p'ansori* (folk opera),

Wŏngak-sa Theater: Cradle of Korean drama

T'okkit'aryŏng (The Song of the Rabbit).

The Wŏngak-sa Theater performed the so-called "new drama," mostly adaptations from new (modern) novels, as early as July 1909.

The Second Period

Following the Wŏngak-sa Theater period, the *Sinp'a* or New-style Plays started in the winter of 1911 with the opening performance of the Hyŏksin-dan (Revolutionary Drama Group) led by Im Sŏng-gu (1887-1921). The group's first presentation was *Heavenly Punishment for the Unfilial*, and the second performance was presented on February 18, 1912 at the Yunhŭng-sa Theater. It was from this time that the so-called *Sinp'a* (the pronunciation being the same either in Japanese or in Korean) was presented to the public.

The play, entitled *The Robber with a Six-Barrel Gun*, was a direct translation from the Japanese *Sinp'a* play, as was the first presentation, but from June of that year the titles and contents of plays were gradually adapted to suit Korean modes and tastes. The Korean theater, in the meantime, outgrew the stage of military and detective plays and from late in 1913 the group performed home tragedies and the love affairs of *kisaeng* girls such as *Konjikiyasha*, or *Changhanmong* in Korean, one of the best of the Japanese *Sinp'a* plays.

Of humble origins, Im Sŏng-gu received no formal education, but charity performances produced by him in order to raise school funds or help beggars earned him considerable respect.

The Hyŏksin-dan Group continued until the spring of 1920. Im died on November 21, 1921.

On the other hand, Yun Paek-nam (1888-1954) organized the Munsusŏng Theater Group on March 29, 1912. This group performed *The Cuckoo*, an adaptation of a Japanese drama, for its first performance at the Wŏngak-sa Theater.

Following that the group gave performances of the best plays of the Japanese *Sinp'a* theater until June, 1916 when it was disbanded.

The Munsusŏng Group began to perform original plays such as *The Youth*, co-authored by Cho Il-che and Yi Ha-mong, and adaptations from such novels serialized in daily newspapers as *The Tear* by Yi Ha-mong. The group, organized by Korean students studying in Tokyo, was called the theater of the intellectuals, but its popularity among the people was, it seems, less than that of the Hyŏksin-dan Group.

The uneducated Im Sŏng-gu organized the Hyŏksin-dan Group of actors of about his own age and performed comparatively low quality works of the Japanese *Sinp'a* theater, while the Munsusŏng, from the first, presented the so-called "literary plays" which made up the top performances of the Japanese *Sinp'a* theater. The popularity of the former was due to another fact — that the level of drama appreciation by Korean audiences of the time was low and so audiences responded with more enthusiasm to the earthy adaptation of Japanese plays into Korean than to the literary translations of the latter group, which in effect tried to transplant the Japanese stage in Korea.

In brief, the two theater groups, which rose and fell almost at the same time during the first half of the so-called period of New-style Plays, had many contrasting aspects as delineated above.

Many other small groups made brief appearances during this period: the Yuil-dan led by Yi Ki-se; the Yesŏng-jwa, an incorporation of the Munsusŏng and the Yuil-dan; the Munye-dan organized by Yi Ki-se; the Kaeryang-jwa and the Sinkŭk-sa of Kim Do-san; the Chwisŏng-jwa of Kim So-rang; Yi Ki-se's Yesul-hyŏphoe (changed to Yesul-jwa) and Yun Paek-nam's Minjung-kŭkdan. The Chwisŏng-jwa had the longest life of them all, until the end of 1929.

The Third Period

The T'owŏl-hoe (Saturday-Monday Society) Dramatic Group, under the leadership of Pak Sŭng-hŭi, played the central role during the 1920's, which might be termed the latter half of the so-called New-style Plays period.

Before the T'owŏl-hoe Group, which was composed entirely of Korean students in Tokyo, gave its first performance in Korea in 1923, it was organized (in 1921) as a students' traveling theatrical group to make a one-and-a-half-month tour of trial performances in Korea during the school vacation. Its repertory consisted of *The Death of Kim Yŏng-il* by Cho Po-suk; *The Last Handshake* by Hong Nan-p'a; and *The Glittering Gate* by Lord Dunsany. Among its members were such persons who made their names in Korea's theatrical world as Hong Hae-sŏng, Kim Su-san, Cho Po-suk and Ma Hae-song.

Although the student drama movement was obviously aimed at general enlightenment as well as at the enhancement of artistic activities, it nevertheless exerted an influence on the commercial theater by forcing it to better performance standards. In this respect, the traveling drama group played a pioneer role. Such students' drama groups as the Songkyŏng Hakhoe and the Caltop Society were a few of the many student theatrical bodies active during that period.

At around that time Hyŏn Chŏl, who graduated from the Actors' Studio affiliated to the Tokyo Academy of Arts, returned to Korea (in 1920) to establish an Academy of Arts, which developed in three years into the Actors' Studio of Korea. The studio presented two trial performances: Henrik Ibsen's *The Doll's House* and Anton Chekhov's *The Bear* and *The Dog*.

Hyŏn Chŏl was a talented and versatile man. He translated *Hamlet* into Korean from the Japanese translations and serialized it in the *Kaebyŏk* magazine and later in 1923 published it. Following this publication, attempts were made to translate Western plays into Korean, for example, Yang

Paek-hwa's translation of Ibsen's *The Doll's House* was published in 1923 and Yi Sang-su's *The Merchant of Venice* and *The Lady of the Sea* were published in 1924.

In 1922 a group of Korean students, including Pak Sŭng-hŭi, Kim Bok-chin, Kim Ki-jin, Yi Su-gu and Kim Ŭl-han, organized the T'owŏl-hoe (Saturday and Monday Society), which in 1923 presented Pak Sŭng-hŭi's original |play, *Kilsik*, Anton Chekhov's *The Bear*, G. B. Shaw's *How She Lied to Her Husband*, and *The Famine*.

The appearance of the T'owŏl-hoe, at a time when the Korean theatrical world was in the throes of rebirth from the so-called New-style Play modes with the import of the modern Western plays, marked a decisive turning point on the Korean stage. Although its first presentation turned to be a flop, its second performance in September of that year proved to be such a smashing success that it is said to have enabled the Korean stage to achieve what it would normally take a few decades. Included in this second presentation were Tolstoy's *Resurrection*, Wilhelm Mayer Forester's *Alt-Heidelberg*, and G. B. Shaw's *How She Lied to Her Husband*. It was also the first attempt to produce modern Western plays on the Korean stage.

From April 1924, the group made a one-year contract with the Kwangmudae Theater, following its reorganization centering around Pak Sŭng-hŭi. From then on it tended to strike a compromise with commercialism as is attested to in its repertory of the time. It took up such favorite plays of the New-style as *Changhanmong* and *Resurrection*, and from 1925 such folkish Korean stories as *Ch'unhyangjŏn, Simch'ŏngjŏn* and *Changhwahongnyŏnjŏn*, and Yi Kwang-su's *Moojŏng (Pitiless)*. The group toured the country for performances from November 1925 to 1931; and in 1932 it changed its name to T'aeyang Theater.

The leader of the group, Pak Sŭng-hŭi, recalls that the number of performances by the T'owŏl-hoe "came to 180 and I|wrote more than 200 plays during that period."

The T'owŏl-hoe, in an effort to do away with the influence of the Japanese *Sinp'a* theater which became rampant here following the days of the Revolutionary Theater Group, tried to revolutionize theatrical form and technique, while preserving the literary value of plays. Even in such minute details as play technique, dialogue, stage setting, and costuming, the group saw to it that production was in line with the realism of modern plays. Anyway, it is safe to say that the T'owŏl-hoe played a pioneer role in paving the way for the new drama movement of the 1930's.

Drama groups active during those periods were, among others, the Chuisung-jwa, the Taeyang Theater (successor to the T'owŏl-hoe), the Chosŏn Yŏnkŭk-sa, the Yŏnkŭk-sijang, the Sinmudae, the Radio Drama Association, and the Chungoe-kŭkjang.

The Fourth Period

A 12-man group organized, in July 1931, the Academy of Theatrical Arts in order to promote the study of dramatic arts and of the new drama movement. Its members included Yun Paek-nam and Hong Hae-sŏng, besides such students of foreign literature as Suh Hang-suk, Kim Chin-sŏp, Yi Ha-yun, Chang Ki-je, Yi Hŭn-gu, Yu Ch'i-jin, Ch'oe Chong-u, Cho Hi-sun, Zŏng In-sŏb and Ham Dae-hun.

The academy sponsored a summer seminar on dramatic arts in August and in November organized the Experimental Theater, a drama group attached to the academy, and held the first lecture meeting in Korea on dramatic arts.

The Experimental Theater presented, on May 5, 1932 Ham Dae-hun's translation of N. Gogol's *The Inspector*, as its first production with Hong Hae-sŏng's (1893-1957) directing. Its second performance consisted of Irving's *The Lover* (translated by Yi Ha-yun), Lady Gregory's *The Prison Gate* (translated by Ch'oe Chŏng-u) and R. Goering's *The Sea War* (translated by Cho Hi-sun). Hong Hae-sŏng directed all of them.

For its third performance the theater produced Yu Ch'i-jin's first play, *The Earthen Hut*, on February 9, 1933. From then until March 1938, when the group was dissolved by the Japanese authorities, the Experimental Theater recorded 17 presentations. Members of the theater later regrouped to form, in corporation with Korean students in Tokyo, the Kŭkyunjwa and performed their 23rd presentation before this group was also disbanded in May 1939 by the Japanese.

Following its formation in 1931, the Experimental Theater devoted itself to producing translated plays by Russian and northern European playwrights as well as the best Irish, English, French and American plays on one hand as a means of paving the way for the establishment of "new drama" in this country, on the other hand, it produced original plays by such Korean playwrights as Yu Ch'i-jin, Yi Mu-yŏng and Yi Kwang-su.

The academy also published a monthly magazine, *Theater Arts*, for four months.

The eight years of trials the Experimental Theater underwent, however, made lasting contributions to the establishment and enhancement of the standards of "new drama" and thus has an important place in the history of Korean dramatic arts.

Student drama activities during those years also deserve attention. The Ewha Womans College produced Shakespeare's *The Merchant of Venice* in November 1929 and again *The Taming of the Shrew* in December 1931. The Chosŏn Christian College (predecessor to Yonsei University) presented Tolstoy's *The Power of Darkness*, Ibsen's *The Lady of the Sea*, Lord Dunsany's *The Tents of Arabia* and John Galsworthy's *Justice*.

Posŏng College (predecessor to Korea University) and Severance Medical College (now incorporated into Yonsei University), and many other boys' and girls' high schools took part in the exciting student drama activities.

The cover of the 2nd issue of *Kūkyesul* (Theater Art).

Another fact that deserves a special mention here was the opening, in November 1935, of the Oriental (*Tongyang*) Theater, for the presentation of drama only. This heralded in a golden period of commercial theater in pace with the new drama movement of the Academy of Theater Arts. The theater operated three attached drama troupes — Chŏng Chun-jwa, Hikŭk-jwa (later Hohwasun) and Tongkŭk-jwa — which made performance tours in turn throughout the country with varied programs ranging from historical plays to such melodramas as domestic tragedies and the love affairs of entertainment girls.

To name only a few of the plays produced during the period, Yi Wun-bang's *The Night at the Borderland*; Ch'oe Dŏk-kyun's *Pathos in the Monk's Quarter* and *Ch'unhyangjŏn*; Yi Kwang su's *Tragic Story of King Tanjong, Love* and *Pitiless*; Yi Sŏ-gu's *The Power of a Mother*; Miss Pak Hwa-sŏng's *The White Flower*; and Im Sŏn-kyu's *Betrayed by Love and Cried Over Money*, etc. These melodramatic plays made up what was called the "higher New-style Play," and brought forth a golden period for the commercial theater until the 1940's when Japanese policy banned the theatrical movement.

The theater was operated under two departments — literary and production — staffed by Ch'oe Dŏk-kyun and Yi Sŏ-gu and Yi Wun-bang, Hong Hae-sŏng and Pak Chin respectively, which jointly took charge of producing plays, which were, however, generally speaking, not necessarily what could be called the best plays. Nevertheless, we cannot ignore its contributions to the history of the Korean theater. Indeed, for the first time since the Kwangmudae Theater of the T'owŏl-hoe, it proved the possibility of operating a special theater for drama only and it also produced many actors and actresses who at present form the nucleus of professional drama troupes and of Korean filmdom.

Other major drama groups active during this period were the Yewŏn-jwa, the Chungang-mudae, the Nangman-jwa, the Kukmin-jwa, the Yŏnkūk-hoe, and the Arang. Some 100 commercial and experimental drama groups, small and large, traveled around the country presenting a wide range of programs from the New-style Plays, new dramas and plays that were a compromise between *Sinp'a* and New Drama, until the beginning of the 1940's, the decade that proved to be the dark age of Korea's cultural life.

With the beginning of the Sino-Japanese War, Japan's increasingly strict control over Korea led to the formation of the Chosŏn (Korean) Theater Association at the end of 1940, which was, in July 1942, reformed into the Chosŏn Cultural Theater Association, to which only 16 drama and 11 musical groups were affiliated with government approval.

The association held its first drama contest in order to establish what it called the "national drama," and five theatrical groups participated in the competition. The second drama contest, which ran for four months from September of 1943, was participated in by eight drama groups. Viewed from the standpoint of Korean national culture, this period was the dark age of the reactionary theater, from which, however, appeared Yu Ch'i-jin's *The Amur River*, Im Sŏn-kyu's *The Village of Camellia* and Kim Tae-jin's *Genghis Khan.*

The Korean theater, which collaborated in spite of itself in perpetuating the reactionary theater movement toward the end of Japanese colonial days, awakened from its nightmare when the country was liberated in 1945, recovered the true nature of a national theater, and prepared itself to advance toward the common goal of post-World War II theater activities.

Yu Ch'i-jin and the Theater of Korea

WILLIAM E. HENTHORN

The playwright-producer Yu Ch'i-jin (Tong-nang by penname) was born in Ch'ungmu City, a small town on an inlet along the craggy, island-strewn southeastern coast of Korea which takes its name from the literary appellation of Yi Sun-sin, the Korean admiral who inflicted heavy casualties on the sixteenth century Japanese invaders with his iron-clad 'Turtle' ships. Yu was born in 1905, the year Japan forced the Protectorate Treaty on Korea and he grew to manhood during the period Korea was a colony of Japan (1910-1945). Following his graduation from normal school in Ch'ungmu City in 1918, he was trained briefly in communications in the bustling commercial seaport of Pusan and for a short time worked in the postal service in Ch'ungmu City. Then, shortly after the bloody suppression of the passive nation-wide independence demonstration of March 1, 1919, Yu was sent to Tokyo to continue his education. There, according to one biographical sketch, he read *Le Théâtre du peuple* (1903) by the French dramatist Romain Rolland (1866-1944) which influenced him toward the study of the theater.

The year before Yu finished his secondary education in Tokyo, the Japanese capital was devastated by the great Tokyo earthquake of 1923. When the tremors ceased rumors began to circulate through the city that Koreans were responsible for the many fires which swept parts of the Japanese capital. Koreans were sought out and butchered on the spot. Yu was eighteen or nineteen at the time.

The next year Yu entered the Department of English Literature at Rikkyo College in Japan, graduating in 1931, the year Japanese military movements began in Manchuria and North China. This would soon bring an end to those literary movements which had begun to develop following the relaxation of Japanese controls in Korea after the 1919 Independence Demonstrations. Yu's graduation thesis, Research on Sean O'Casey, published serially in the Journal of English-American Literature, *Ei-Bei Bungaku,* is often mentioned when this period of Korean literary activity is compared to the 'Irish Renaissance.' Yu returned to the Korean capital after his graduation where he and others organized the Theatrical Arts Research Society, *Kŭgyesul yŏn'gu-hoe.* He became active in the operational arm of the Society, the Experimental Theater, *Silhŏm mudae,* playing minor roles in the group's 1932 presentations of Ham Tae-hun's translation of Gogol's *The Inspector General* and Chang Ki-je's translation of Shaw's *Arms and the Man.* In this year Yu wrote his first play, *The Earthen Hut* (2 acts), the first Korean production of the Experimental Theater. It was to mark the beginning of a new era in Korean theater.[1] In an article published in the literary monthly *Hyŏndae munhak,* Yu reflects on his life as a playwright which commenced at that time.

> When I was young, I was physically weak and my spirit was weak also. While I was attending a normal school—I was about eleven or twelve at the time—I heard stories of earthquakes and tidal waves from the teachers. When an earthquake occurred, the world would shake and the earth would split open. When a tidal wave suddenly arose, the waters of the ocean would rise and sweep away whole city blocks of people. After I heard this, I lost my appetite for food for the entire day—it was a time to face the wall and cry. It was unbearable to think people lived on this uneasy globe which itself trembled and shook.
>
> Even while I, fragile of limb and spirit, grew strong, I was always seized anew by anxiety and terror and this became a

chronic illness. Even in the emotion of love toward the opposite sex, I could not wash myself free of this uneasy feeling toward death. And so I, who had no philosophy, became a philosopher and tried to solve the inexplicable, original enigma of death. I ransacked books on literature and decided to enter the Department of Literature in the University but even here I found no satisfactory explanation for this anxiety. Finally, I arrived at the startling conclusion that life is nothing and it is senseless and without meaning to think of the meaning of life. And yet, inside this negative, gray fog, I obtained one compass-needle as a guide to this perplexing life. That was, if my past life was already a cipher and like the air, then I would take the road of a valuable death by selecting an intoxicating life. I made up my mind — even from the doorway of the Department of Arts — to study 'something extremely utilitarian, the theater.

In thought, I found myself at the time in sympathy with the strife-filled doctrines of Anarchism. This was about the time, I believe, that I entered Rikkyo College, about thirty years ago. After that, as soon as I finished school, I returned to Seoul and together with Kim Chin-sŏp, Kim Kwang-sŏp, Ch'oe Chŏng-u, Chang Ki-je, Yi Ha-yun, Chŏng In-sŏp, Hong Hae-sŏng, So Hang-sŏk, Yun Paeng-nam, Ham Tae-hun, and Pak Yŏng-hi organized the Theatrical Arts Research Society. In the summer of 1931, we took the first step of the practical theater movement. And, with the production of my drama *The Earthen Hut* by this company my first voyage as a playwright began.

The Earthen Hut was produced by Hong Hae-sŏng at the Public Meeting Hall, *konghoedang* in the Sogong-dong district in February 1933. It was staged with scenery and props by Yu Hyŏng-mok with the actor Yi Ung and the actress Kim Yŏng-ok playing the lead roles. The poet Kim Kwang-sŏp played the part of Samjo brilliantly. Since this drama has been included in the collection of my plays, *Cow,* there are probably those among the readers who have read it; yet, it was, to say the least, a difficult work and looking at it now it seems embarrassingly dull.

In spite of that, it caused great excitement among the

audience at the time. No sooner had the final curtain come down, together with the sound of applause like thunder, a portion of the audience thronged to the actors' dressing rooms (since the dressing rooms at the Public Meeting Hall had not been completed, the dressing rooms were provided by a curtain strung to one side of the spectator's seats), and the rush to find the author and bring him out left me, not elated but at a loss what to do. It gave the other members of the Theatrical Arts Research Society more happiness than it did me.

My excitement subsided and I returned home but I couldn't sleep. My heart pounded like a bridegroom on the first night of his honeymoon. *The Earthen Hut* captured the hearts of the audience to this extent, not from any artistic quality of the work but rather from the excitement of a situation which drew from an audience starving, in a period of sick reality, for their own self expression.

Works which formed a link with *The Earthen Hut* were: *View of a Village with Willows*, staged by the Society at *the* Chōsen Keikijō in November 1933; *Streets of the Poor*, performed in Tokyo in 1934 at the Tsukiji Little Theater by the March 1st Troupe, *Sam-il kūkchang*; and *Cow*, run serially in the newspaper *Tong-A Ilbo* in 1934. In these works I described the tragedy of our life under the pressures of the circumstances of the times as they actually were. However, the Japanese police would not allow me to continue such themes any longer. The work *Cow* brought trouble and I was arrested and held in the Chongno Police Station.* This brought with it a temporary change in my life as a playwright. That is, I sought the theme of my work in the humanistic emotions of love rather than in the actual conditions of real life. Works which belong to this period are: Donkey, *Tangnagwi* published in serial form in the *Chosŏn Ilbo* newspaper in 1935; *Time of Mourning*, performed by the Kugyŏnjwa troupe in November 1935; *The Sisters*, staged by the Kugyŏnjwa at the Pumin'gwan Theater in May 1936; *Married Couple* published in the literary magazine *Munjang* in 1941.

---

*Arrested were Yu, Pak Tong-wŏn, and Yi Hae-ryang, all members of the Students' Art Company, *Haksaeng Yesul-jwa* which had included the play *Cow* in their repertoire. They were held over three months without charge.

As my position as a writer at the time was a type of escape, my works had already lost their elastic force, which was unavoidable. My dark period continued for a while but the flame in my heart was by no means extinguished. On the contrary, as time passed it began to burn deeper inside me until it was as though I had pleurisy. That is, this 'fire' concealed in my veins now made me feel a certain anger even for the Realism in which I had placed my trust and which had been my principle as a playwright. I acquired a dislike for the works of writers like Anton Chekhov, Synge, and Sean O'Casey after whom I had patterned myself. This was because their contemplative world could not soothe the 'fire' in my heart in the least. Therefore, I began a reexamination of the works of writers like Shakespeare, Moliere and others who belonged to the period before Naturalism. And here I found a partial answer. This is the manner in which I came to propose the necessity in our literary world for romanticism based upon Realism. That period was, moreover, a time when the left-wing critics were wagging their heads — if the first said "Realism" the second would say "Realism" — so there were not just a few who opposed my suggestion. I replied to their opposition in this manner. Here is an extract of my view which was published in the newspaper at the time:

'The *Romanticism* of which I speak is not an absorption in fantasy, the enjoyment of peach-colored dreams isolated from the reality of the 20th century. Perhaps if one were to advocate dreaming such dreams in this age then it would be an error of an era. In general our intelligentsia belong inescapably to the class of the petite bourgeois. Our actual circumstances are both dismal and wretched. If we examine the works produced in this realistic life, we find there is no hope, there is no way to find relief. There is only an unpleasant, flowing monotone of darkness and that is all. I couldn't be the only one who has had this experience, nor could I be the only one who has stamped his feet in frustration hoping to be rescued from this. Practically all of the works introduced into the Korean literary stream are of this hue. However, it will not do for the writer to lose this wrestling match with reality. For there is nothing that says that humanity must perish because reality is such that it is difficult to exist.'

The writer's hope is the 'fire' that is in his heart. Before the corpse of the idea from this fire is buried in reality we must let it stand for itself. We must allow it to soar. If we do not, it will be lost forever in the turgid stream of reality.

This appeared in the *Maeil Sinbo* newspaper in January 1938. With this pet theory in hand I chose for my initial productions works which vividly portrayed a desire for life. Namely, works — all performed by the Kugyŏnjwa troupe at the Pumin'gwan Theater — DuBose Heyward's *Porgy* (1925) performed in January 1937 and Maxwell Anderson's *Winterset* (1935) performed in 1938.

I produced these with the intention of studying, as a playwright, the spirit of Romanticism as I saw it, using the foreign writers as a mirror. And, in my own works such as the dramatization of *The Prince in Hempen Clothing and the Princess of Loyang*, *The Story of Ch'unhyang*, etc., I endeavored to place my own emphasis in the work.

Conditions were such at the time — the Japanese occupation grew severe — that the pressure was extreme so we could not possibly take up the scalpel against the actual conditions under which we lived. For this reason, as a writer, I had no recourse but to set the scene in a distant period as in works like *The Prince in Hempen Clothing* . . . and *The Story of Ch'unhyang*. And this is rather regrettable for it could only be termed humiliating. Yet, the actual conditions of the time created a situation from which we could not escape.

However, following the liberation, I obtained the opportunity to experiment with this idea. And I here confess that I wrote the following from the preparations of a writer's feelings in a humble attempt to produce a 'spirit of romance' based upon the 'real': *The Drum Which Beat Itself* written in 1946; *The Milky Way*, 1947; *Cry of Anguish*, 1952; *I Want to Become a Human Being*, 1953; *The Green Sage*, 1954, and, what's worse, even *Fatherland*, written in 1946.

While the past has been a traditional source of literary inspiration, aside from the fact that the general story and theme of historical plays are common knowledge which makes new interpretations even more meaningful, Yu's remarks give us a better view of some of the influences on the development of modern Korean historical drama. Yu's plays *The Earthen Hut, Cow, Cry of Anguish, Yu Kwan-sun* and *The Han River Flows* reflect the great sense of tragedy and loss which have been the bitter legacy of the immediate past with its occupation, wars, rapid social change, and the loss of things held dear, while works like *The Story of Ch'unhyang, The Six Who Died*, and *The Song of Ch'ŏyong* drawn from the ancient past seem to be, in the tradition of Joyce, a struggle to forge a new national conscience; a search through the distant and shadowed centuries of history and legend and myth for respect, pride, dignity, and hope. Intimately related, perhaps even inseparable, is the struggle for balance between Realism and Romanticism even in Yu's works and of which he speaks in his article, for the opposition of the real and the romantic is the story of life itself and brings to mind Hemingway's remark: "We are all standing in the mud only some of us are looking at the stars." Yu Ch'i-jin was such a man.

BIBLIOGRAPHY

The Plays of Yu Ch'i-jin (to 1959)

    The dates generally represent performance or publication dates rather than completion of a work.

1932 — The Earthen Hut, *T'omak* (2 acts)
1933 — View of a Village with Willows, *Pŏdŭnamu sŏn tongniŭi p'unggyŏng* (1 act)
1934 — Cow, *So* (3 acts)
    — Street of the Poor, *Pinmin'ga;* also known by the title Under the Rooftops of Seoul, *Sŏurŭi chibung mit*
1935 — Donkey, *Tangnagwi* (1 act)
    — Time of Mourning, *Chesa*
1936 — The Sisters, *Chamae* (3 acts)
    — Record of an Abundant Year, *P'ungnyŏn'gi;* a rewritten version of *Cow*

1938 — Mt. Kaegol, *Kaegol-san* (5 acts); title changed to The Prince in Hempen Clothing and the Princess of Loyang, *Maūi t'aeja wa Nangnang kongju,* in 1943.
1941 — The Jujube Tree, *Taech'u-namu* (4 acts)
— The Amur River, *Hūgyong-gang*
— The Married Couple, *Pubu*
1946 — Fatherland, *Choguk* (1 act)
— The Drum Which Beat Itself, *Chamyŏnggo* (5 acts)
1950 — Wŏnsul, *Wŏnsullang* (5 acts)
— Whither?, *Ōdiro*
— The Death of the Magpies, *KKach'iŭi chugūm* (2 scenes)
(The first scene of this play has been translated by S. E. Solberg and is included in *Korea Through Her Arts,* Seoul, 1965.)
— With the Fatherland, the Verdant Spring, *Ch'ŏngch'unŭn choguk-kwa tōburō* (1 act)
— Milky Way, *Ūnhasu* (3 acts)
— Star, *Pyŏl* (5 acts)
1953 — Song of Ch'ŏyong, *Ch'ŏyongŭi norae* (4 acts)
— The Kaya Harp, *Kayagūm* (4 acts)
— Cry of Anguish, *T'onggok* (4 acts)
— Partition, *Changbyŏk* (1 act)
— I too Want to Become a Human Being, *Nado in'gani toeryŏnda*
1955 — The Green Sage, *P'urūn sŏngin* (4 acts)
— The Six Who Died, *Sayuksin*
1957 — The Tragic History of King Tanjong *Tanjong aesa;* a dramatization of a novel of the same name by Y'i Kwang-su.
— Why Fight?, *Wae ssawŏ?;* a rewritten version of *The Jujube Tree*
1958 — The Han River Flows, *Han'gangūn hūrūnda* (22 scenes)
— Yu Kwan-sun

COLLECTIONS

— Collected Dramas of Yu Ch'i-jin, *Yu Ch'i-jin Hūigok-chip.* 1951
— A Collection of Historical Plays by Yu Ch'i-jin, *Yu Ch'i-jin Yŏksagūk-chip.* 1951.
— *Wŏnsullang.* 1953.
— I too Want to Become a Human Being. 1953.
— Selected Dramas of Yu Ch'i-jin, *Yu Ch'i-jin Hūigok Sŏnjip.* 1957.
— Complete Collection of Korean Literature, Vol. 32, *Han'guk Munhak Chŏnjip.*

NOTES

1. Professor Forrest Pitts of the University of Hawaii has informed me of the following doctoral dissertation: Cho Oh-kon, *Yu Ch'i-jin: A Patriotic Playwright of Korea.* Dissertations Abstracts International 33 (March 1973). 352 pp. 5334-A. UN No. 73-5344.

   An English language summary of the history of the Korean theater is included in Yi Tu-hyōn, *Han'guk sin'gūksa yōn'gu,* Seoul: Seoul National University Press, 1966.
2. See David Y. Chen, "The Trilogy of Ts'ao Yü and Western Drama," *Asia and the Humanities,* Indiana University, Bloomington, Indiana, 1959, pp. 27-37.

Projection of Tradition in Modern Drama

Yu MIN-YŎNG

The modern drama of Korea made its debut with Japan's invasion of the peninsula. Thus, Japan served as the intermediary and catalyst of the modern Korean drama. The so-called *Sinp'a* (new school) theater which began in 1911 was an exact copy of the Japanese new school that came into being in Japan toward the close of the 19th century. The orthodox modern drama of the West burgeoning in the early 1920s was also transmitted to Korea via Japan. It therefore was an indirect acceptance with some refraction.

Korea's modern drama that had emerged in this fashion kept growing and took root with little soul-searching until the nation was liberated from Japan in 1945. Korean theater flowed in two main streams: the one, *Sinp'a* drama, featuring highly sentimental, didactic and popular themes and the other, the orthodox new drama, seeking to absorb the realism of modern Western drama.

Following liberation Korean theater had to operate under the strain of the ideological rivalry between the right wing and the left wing as well as the partition of the territory into the south and the north. With the Korean War of 1950 as a turning point most leading members of the commercial *Sinp'a* group went over to north Korea where they provided the foundation for the dramatic art in the communist society. On the other hand, south Korea was the venue for the realism-oriented drama devoted to pure and orthodox theater. The territorial division of the country entailed division of drama, too.

The diametrical difference in the official ideologies of the two parts resulted in developing drama in different directions. Those in north Korea produced the so-called revolutionary drama by infusing socialistic realism into the *Sinp'a* prototype, thereby turning plays into an instrument of socialist political propaganda. In south Korea the remnants of the *Sinp'a* theater were largely cleared as a result of the war. Nevertheless, its dramatic circles remained lethargic and unproductive for some time in the midst of an extremely conservative social milieu in the 1950s.

However, as popular demand for recovering cultural identity began to surge in the early 1960s, an increasing number of attempts were made to produce nationalistic drama — a modernized version of drama inspired by Korean perspective and enacted in a Korean style.

Though their contents and forms varied widely, both south and north Korea passed the stage of sticking to the *Sinp'a* tradition left over from Japanese colonialism and mere immitation of the Western modern drama to look farther beyond.

O Yŏng-jin was the leading figure in initiating a movement for *Minjokgŭk* (nationalistic drama) in Korea. In the 1960s many other playwrights and stage producers joined him. It grew increasingly popular and better organized as a group movement in the 1970s, forming a central stream in Korean theater.

Aimed at exploring an independent and unique outlet of dramatic expression for the Korean people, the movement tried to inject the Korean tradition into the contents and forms of modern drama. There is nothing unnatural about it. However, we can hardly deny the existence of undramatic factors which prompt the projection of our tradition into our theater. The rigidity of the political situation in which freedom of expression was limited prevented writers and producers from criticizing reality point-blank. Under the circumstances, they discovered some raw material and inspiration in the history and traditional customs of the nation, and made subdued criticism. It encouraged a trend toward localism. The situation was quite similar to the one which had existed in the closing years of Japanese colonialism.

The movement for nationalistic drama begun by O Yŏng-jin was carried over by a group of youthful, mostly in their thirties, playwrights spearheaded by O T'ae-sŏk—Ch'oe In-hun, Yun Tae-sŏng, Pak Sŏng-jae, Yi Ŏn-ho, Yi Pyŏng-wŏn and Chang So-hyŏn. Their dramatic creation is characterized by a heavy reliance on themes and motifs drawn from traditional folklore and old literature.

Traditional folklore includes myths, folktales, legends, folksongs, shamanistic rites, mask plays, *P'ansori* (Korean opera), puppet plays and popular customs; old literature consists of novels, poems and lyrics. O Yŏng-jin, for example, started with folktales, dealt extensively with rites of passage and then went on to reinterpret and recreate old novels from a modern standpoint.

He omitted from the rites of passage only the coming-of-age ceremony because of its ritual simplicity. Other rites related to wedding, funeral and ancestor-worship were all made subjects of his various plays. *Maengjinsadaek kyŏngsa* or the Wedding Day is a dramatization of the nuptial rite; *Paebaeng'i kut* (scenario) is a dramatization of the funeral rites and *Hannaeŭi sŭngch'ŏn* (Ascension of Hannae) is a dramatization of ancestor-worship rituals. They constitute a trilogy.

Old novels were rendered into satires in *Hŏsaeng-jŏn* and *Naŭi dangsin*. *Hŏsaeng-jŏn* is based on novels by Pak Chi-wŏn (18th century) entitled *Hŏsaengwŏn-jŏn* and *Yangban-jŏn*. *Naŭi dangsin* is a modernistic version of *Onggojib-jŏn*.

Subjects adopted from a folktale and a legend are used in such works as *His Excellency Yi Chung-saeng Is Still Alive* and the *Ascension of Hannae*. In accepting tradition, O Yŏng-jin claims that he had four objectives in mind: 1. recreation of a typical personality type; 2. esthetic regeneration of the contents of drama involving satire and humor; 3. revival of such formalistic elements as music and dance; 4. reexamination of the contents, forms and techniques of traditional theater (including the epic style evident in *P'ansori*).

He, therefore, searches out a typical personality out of old novels and makes a caricature of modern man who becomes more and more perverted and dwarfed. By restoring the outstanding dramatic nature of traditional arts today, he seeks to give fresh integrity to the man and theater of today which have been dominated by Japanese and Western influence.

O's world of art is preoccupied with a satire on alien influence. Such an approach seems quite relevant. What was gained from his majoring in Korean literature is reflected in his script full of rhythmical dialogue occurring frequently in old Korean novels and *P'ansori*. The atmosphere of his plays is rich in indigenous flavor.

O T'ae-sŏk and Yun Tae-sŏng were a little different. Unlike O who was engaged in deriving from and accepting things innate in tradition, the two young writers with only weak grounding in Korean literature or folklore seemed to be obsessed with the external and visible forms. Therefore, their source of material was comparatively limited to forms of shaman rites and folk theater.

As for Yun Tae-sŏng, his plays *Mangnani* (Executioner) and *Nobi-munsŏ* (Slave certificates) were intended for mask play. While these two works were successful in satirizing reality, they were less so in dramatic effect. Only *Nŏdomŏkko mullŏnara* (You get away with it) based on the exorcist rite of *Changdaejangdae kut* native to Hwanghae Province was a success. The play was to be enacted in a private yard through the medium of shamanistic rituals by way of bitterly criticizing the social blights and moral decadence of today.

O T'ae-sŏk uses a much wider scope and variety of subjects

than Yun Tae-sŏng. His scope is as wide as O Yŏng-jin's. As far as techniques are concerned, O T'ae-sŏk is more empirical and bold than O Yŏng-jin. At first, he tried to transplant the external forms of puppet plays and mask plays to the modern drama he created. Then, he gradually extended his area of interest to cover such old customs and primitive rituals as funeral services or shaman exorcism.

His script "Grafting" with a subtitle of "a play for puppets" was meant for simple aboriginal puppets. It is his first attempt at projecting tradition into contemporary times. His second script was *Soettugi nori* — an adaptation of a folk puppet play. In it he tried to rebuild the text of Korea's traditional puppet play, *Sandae nori* of Yangju, around a plot supplied by *La Fourberie de Scapain*, a comedy by Moliere. *Soettugi nori* in which he attempted to graft the theater of East and West turned out to be another failure.

An approach to things traditional in terms of form, not of substance, is bound to fail. This was demonstrated clearly by O T'ae-sŏk as was the case with Yun Tae-sŏng. The failure illustrated the difficulty of rendering a modern drama into an old-fashioned puppet play or combining the forms of heterogeneous Eastern and Western theater. Having suffered two failures, O T'ae-sŏk began to approach the contents, instead of the external form. *Ch'obun* (Grass tomb) represents the initial materialization of such an endeavor.

Grass tomb is a peculiar institution of disposing of a dead body surviving in some islands off the southern coast. It employed the funeral rites as theme to symbolize the destruction of ethics and order as a result of environmental degradation caused by contemporary civilization. Problems of life and death are dealt with by means of awesome rituals.

His relative success in approaching the inner aspect made up for his failure in his approach to the external aspect. He then jumped into the world of old customs and novels. To be exact, he broadened his horizon, rather than jumped into it. Against the background two scripts were born: one was *Yakjangsa*

(The Drug Peddler) depicting the loquacious storyteller in the street; the other was *Ch'unp'ungŭi ch'ŏ* (Wife of *Ch'unp'ung*) adapted from an old novel titled *Yi ch'unp'ung-jŏn*.

Since early times there were in Korea two kinds of professional vagrant storytellers: The one was *Chŏnkisu* who specialized in peddling tales and the other was the medicine peddler. *Yakjangsa* by O is a satire on the prevailing conditions of society as seen through the life of a traveling drug dealer. *Ch'unp'ungŭi ch'ŏ* reproduced in part the plot and characters of the old novel *Yi ch'unp'ung-jŏn* but the whole contents are much different from those of the latter. It is a comedy written in a most impulsive and intuitive way to portray the irregularities and absurdities of the present-day world.

Of late O T'ae-sŏk seems to be delving deeper. Going beyond the realm of improvisation and talkativeness, he probes the inner world of man. In *Mulbora* (spray of water) he describes the primitive life and affection of men by elaborating on *Kop'uri*, a symbolic ritual procedure of *Ssitkimkut* or *Oku kut*, both shamanistic rites remaining in some southern coastal areas. *Kop'uri* is a procedure through which the dead spirit is sent to the other world. He superimposes the desires and lust of men on such a superstitious happening.

In 1979 O wrote a script titled *Sach'ungi* (Recurrent adolescence). It was since described as *Hanjungnok* (a biographical sketch of the life of the dowager of Prince *Sado*) of the present time. The work deals with marital disharmony between a middle-aged couple and the feeling of grudge (*han*) prevalent among Korean women. *Hangjungnok* was an autobiographical account of the life of Mrs. Hong who had her husband Prince *Sado* murdered and suffered under the oppressive father-in-law, King Yŏngjo. It well portrays *han* (m) of a suffering woman. In depicting a contemporary middle-aged woman, the author interspersed the script with melodious passages from *Hanjungnok* or *Choch'immun* (a tribute to the needle), folk songs or *P'ansori*. They serve to make the entire script an outstanding modern play.

There is another playwright, Ch'oe In-hun, who used to concentrate on novels and switched to writing plays different from O T'ae-sŏk. Beginning with *"Where Shall I Meet You and What Shall I Be?"* which was a dramatic adaptation of the story of Ondal the fool, hero of an age-old folk tale, he established himself as dramatist with *Yennal yejŏgge huŏihuŏi* (Once upon a time, hush and hush) which was based on the legend of a young general in P'yŏngan Province.

He produces one play every year. The third one was *"When It's Springtime in the Fields and Hills,"* a story about the pathetic love affair of a leprous couple. The fourth one was *Tungdungnangnangdung*, based on the story of Prince *Hodong* and Princess *Nangnang* in the *Koguryŏ* period. His earlier plays included *"O, Moon, Moon, A Bright Moon,"* the story of the dutiful *Simch'ŏng*

His primary concern is in the tragic fate of Koreans who are impoverished, exploited and oppressed. He gathers ideas from folktales. In many respects, he is often regarded as similar to the postwar Japanese writer Junji Kinoshita. They are the ones in attempting bitter criticism of power and material civilization by means of themes collected from folktales.

Sometimes he breaks away from the world of fictional folktale and seeks to rebuild it. In the case of the story of *Simch'ŏng*, he reversed the plot to turn its happy ending into an unhappy ending. The original story had it that the dutiful daughter sacrifices herself in the sea in return for grain offerings to Buddha devoted to curing her blind father but she transforms into a flower upon drowning and later becomes a queen of China. Such a happy ending is intended to encourage filial piety. On the contrary, playwright Ch'oe presents *Simch'ŏng* as a prostitute in China who loses her eyesight later. He thus brings the predicament of history into relief.

Similar plays such as *Sadangnae* by Yi Pyŏng-wŏn and *"What Will I Be?"* by Pak Sŏng-jae used as their material

Sadangp'ae (a circle of vagrant performers) or *Changsŭng* (totem poles in front of a village). Some mask plays were also attempted by new writers.

We find in *Minyegŭkchang* troupe a group movement to explore new dimensions in Korean theater. Led by Hŏ Kyu who is deeply committed to inheriting tradition, the group often tries to develop Korean operetta by learning mask dance and traditional folk songs and *P'ansori*. Its members strive to integrate modern drama and traditional folk drama in a bold manner. They attracted much attention by presenting *Muldoridong*, a dramatization of the legend of Hŏ doryŏng involving *Hahoe* mask dance native to North Kyŏngsang Province and *Seoul Multtugi*, a modernized rendition of mask play. Failing in their initial effort at integration of forms, they recently turned to effect an integration of contents.

Their endeavor culminated in *Tasiragi*, a prize-winning entry in the National Drama Festival in 1979. *Tasiragi* is a popular game-ritual related to funeral services in the neighborhood of Chindo in southern Kore. It is an outstanding folk game-ritual juxtaposing life and death. Ho Kyu exhibited excellent techniques in reproducing the old motif in a modern milieu without any compulsiveness. It goes to the credit of the troupe members as well as the playwright and producer that such a play achieved a remarkable success. It owed decisively to the mastery and ensemble of folk music, folk dance, traditional folk song and *Ch'ang* as performed by the members.

The theater movement of Korea has now entered a new phase, breaking away from the indiscriminate immitation and copying of either the new-school drama of Japan or the modern drama of the West. It embodies a determination to evolve a unique form of modern drama for Korea.

Eradication of the remnants of Japanese colonial rule was the first task for the Korean theater. The second task is to resist Western drama. The third will be to create a national theater. This does not mean that we should reject universality. We are just looking for a right path to follow as a member of the Third

World. To do that, it is necessary to wander about the jungle of tradition that is the repository of our national art. In it we should discover our own world and dramatic esthetics.

Maengjinsadaek Kyŏngsa by O Yŏng-jin

Tasiragi by Hŏ Kyu

T'ae (The Womb) by O T'ae-sŏk

Ch'obun (The Grass Tomb) by O T'ae-sŏk

Ch'unp'ungŭi ch'o (The Wife of Ch'unp'ung) by O T'ae-sŏk

Yakchangsa (The Drug Peddler) by O T'ae-sŏk

When it's Springtime in the Fields and Hill by Ch'oe In-hun

O, Moon, Moon, A Bright Moon by Ch'oe In-hun

American Drama in Korea, 1945-1970:

A *Study of Literary and Theatrical Responses**

YOH SUK-KEE

The 'New Theatre' in Korea, as a form of Westernized culture uprooted from traditional drama, emerged around the year 1910. During the following decade, the dominant influence came from the Japanese *Simpa* which literally means a 'new school,' though the term is highly misleading in so far as the newness is questioned in terms of the modern Western theatre. Then, in the 1920s, the first flow of Western realistic drama was seen on the Korean stage. Though the attempt at domestication of European drama at this early stage was sporadic and far from productive, the general tide had already turned in favor of modern realism. And then in the decade following 1930, the literary-oriented theatre of Korea (apart from the successfully popular-commercial ventures) relied heavily upon Western realistic masterpieces such as *A Doll's House, Inspector General, Power of Darkness, Cherry Orchard,* and *The Lower Depth,* to mention some of the plays performed. One can readily surmise the general direction of the enlightened theatre in those days. However, the American drama was an exception to this list of initial sources of inspiration for the new Korean theatre — it remained virtually unknown to most Korean directors until 1937 when the production of Dubose Hayward's *Porgy and Bess* was first attempted in Seoul. The reason this particular play was selected for a Korean audience, remains obscure, since the selection of Western plays previously performed seems to have been based on the principle of a high reputation as modern classics on the stage, and this play was not of such a high reputation even among modern American plays. Reportedly, the director's initial interests were focused on the theme of back consciousness set against white and the non-verbal, folk-operatic elements.

This production was followed immediately by Maxwell Anderson's *Winterset* and then, by Clifford Odets' *Awake and Sing,* both of which were very recent plays and the authors virtually unknown at that time. What such a mode of reception signifies is that no systematic information on American drama had been provided beforehand at all. One remarkable exception is the case of the critic Kim Woo-jin who had earlier introduced Eugene O'Neill as one of the "New contemporary playwrights in the World." The series of articles he wrote as early as 1926 were concerned with Luigi Pirandello and Karel Capek as well as with O'Neill, in which he discussed his plays, *Beyond the Horizon, Anna Christie, The Hairy Ape,* and *Desire Under the Elms,* with both a profound knowledge and keen critical insight unparalleled among Koreans at that time, and even in later years till Korea was liberated by the Allied Forces in 1945.

In the early years of the American military rule over Korea, cultural contacts which Koreans had with the U.S. were mostly peripheral; cheap paperbound editions of popular pulp fiction salvaged from the Army garbage disposal, a handy pocket-sized edition of *Time* magazine, or *The Stars and Stripes.* The memory is still green of those rare chances when I came across a stained copy of *For Whom the Bell Tolls,* or a torn-off paperback copy of *Death of a Salesman* from a heap of rubbish in the crowded South Gate market. Moreover, despite the increasing degree of mutual amity between the two nations, the language barrier seemed almost insuperable and the educational facilities were hardly available to help open a regular channel of cultural transplantation. During those five years from the Liberation to the outbreak of the Korean War, all in all, nine modern American plays were presented on stage, of which two were undoubtedly left-over from the meager pro-war productions. And of the remaining seven, five plays were performed in one year, 1949. These plays — *The Patriots* by Sidney Kingley, *The House of the Brave* by Arthur Laurents, *Watch on the Rhine* by Lillian Hellman, and *Tomorrow the World* and *Deep are the Roots*, both by Gow and D'usseau — all had, interestingly enough, in common one overall theme, that is, a tribute to the ideal of American Democracy, as it is displayed in the homeland or on the battlefield or over racial and ideological conflicts. Although many American plays in this vein could easily be found during and after World War II, the happy coincidence thus witnessed in Korea may well suggest the uses the theater is likely to be put to for the propagation of a cause. Some of the plays had probably been suggested and financed for performing by the U.S. Information Agency, and others given by the Koreans themselves who were eager to be indoctrinated in the newly oriented ideal of Western democracy. Thus in a sense, the first contact that the Korean theatre had with American plays in this period was highly suggestive of the direction of Korean-American relations at the very beginning. Another indicator we could get from these productions is the time, the year 1949, which fact implies that regular presentation of American plays barely started before the devastating military invasion put an end to the early promise. Therefore, the discussion of Korean responses to American drama should inevitably start from the post-Korean War years.

Translations of American Plays

As for the major playwrights such as O'Neill, Wilder, Williams, Miller and Inge, a considerable portion of their important works have been translated into Korean, either in published form or as scripts for the theatre. Even a few of the representative American playwrights are widely known through translation. For example, 8 out of 10 full-length plays written by Tennessee Williams prior to 1960 are available in Korean, while 5 out of 7 plays by Arthur Miller prior to 1968 and 3 out of 5 by William Inge prior to 1959 have been translated; almost the entire set of O'Neill's early one-acters about sea life were put into Korean, so that they have been available widely for the use of college students' dramatic activities and also are one of the most favorite repertories. Such a phenomenon is rather exceptional in a country like Korea where the undertaking of having scripts published, whether in book form or in literary journals, is quite dubious.

Moreover, the chances of other Western plays (except Shakespeare) being translated are relatively rare. Several reasons could be cited for such an unusually favorable acceptance of American drama. The first one is that close contact with the U.S., cultural or otherwise, has made it easier for the Korean public to accept and understand American drama. Secondly, the general standard and quality of American drama, especially of some of the post-war playwrights, easily appealed to the taste of Korean playgoers; for example, *Our Town* (Wilder), *The Glass Menagerie* (Williams), and *Death of a Salesman* (Miller) have been widely read and performed by both professionals and amateur groups. Thirdly, cultural influences exercised by a group of college professors in English departments were potentially strong enough to lead the student-audience interest towards American drama. The English department itself has been one of the most popular academic institutions in American-dominated contemporary Korean society. These potential influences were extended to professional productions: to cite a model case, the late Prof. O Hwa-Sŏp of Yonsei University in Seoul translated as many as 14 American plays during this period (including 5 O'Neills, 3 Wilders, 2 Hellmans and 2

Williamses), all of which were performed either on his own initiative or in close cooperation with professional companies. Under his influence, Yonsei Dramatic Club, a well-known student drama society, presented a total of 15 American plays during the period 1955-1965 (the average number of plays performed in a year is 2). Fourthly, one cannot overlook or underrate the role played by the USIS Book Translation Project which has been giving financial aid to the publication of American plays in translation. And last but not least, there is another striking factor which we can hardly fail to notice, that is, the Koreans' preference for modern Western plays. It is sometimes surprising to see how they feel at home with those alien-born gestures and movements through the medium of which they think they can find some answers to the quest of human mystery as well as emotive pleasures, if somewhat inadequate to their satisfaction.

The Literary-academic Approach

Compared with the relative importance of translated texts in the process of cultural transplantation, research activities on campus were in general slight and hardly productive. Quite contrary to the degree of literary attention paid to contemporary American poets and novelists, the dramatists have been more a classroom and theatre subject than themes for treatises. The one exception is Eugene O'Neill. For the last fifteen years, no less than 16 research theses on his works were submitted to graduate schools in Korea for Master's degrees. This figure seems to be fairly impressive because of the degree of popularity it indicates among the graduate students of American literature whose interest in it usually reflects the trend of literary taste in contemporary Korean society. For comparison, a few statistics will suffice: O'Neill ranks second only to Hemingway who comes first with 19 articles, the third being Hawthorne (10), and next come both Melville and

Twain with only 3 articles each. Steinbeck whose popularity has been well proven by general readers through translation, fares unexpectedly poorly with graduate students with only one thesis so far. (The figures are all based on the bibliographical data compiled at the American Studies Institute of Korea University). Moreover, these O'Neill theses disclose a variety of interest in the dramatist himself, his individual works, the dramatic techniques involved, and methods of approach. For example, there are, among others, such titles as "the Archetypes of Greek Tragedy in his Works," "the Aside and Soliloquy in *Strange Interlude*," and "the Image of Moter Earth in *The Great God Brown*."

Such popularity in the study of O'Neill has its reasons. One explanation is that he was a prolific author and one can comparatively easily trace the transfiguration of the dramatist as he went through different phases of his works. For a research treatise, both his content and style allow a variety of approaches which it seems (but is not really) rather simple and easy for the students to take up in the early stages of their research activities. Some literary-dramatic approaches, such as expressionistic or psychoanalytical, attracted them as they were first being initiated into a world of dramatic interpretation.

But, apart from the critical approach of the literature oriented senior students, the general attitude towards O'Neill in Korea has been much more naive; many found in him a tragic (one may say pseudo-tragic) vision of life which they could easily sympathize with. As one researcher of Korean student dramatic activities has pointed out: "Finding in the world of O'Neill's works an essential tragic quality of a wandering soul searching for the ideal, younger generations of this country quickly responded to his appeal. This explains one reason why O'Neill has been staged and appreciated much more frequently by student groups than by professionals. Moreover, some of the recurring themes in his plays — conflict among the members of a family, the problem of adolescence, social ethics on the decline — were so akin to the issues raised in Korean plays that further intimacy was affirmed by Korean spectators." (Kim Sung-A, "A Study of Student Dramatic Activities in Korea," 1971)

Theatrical Response

As for performance frequences, several statistical figures agree that the ratio of American plays performed during this period considerably outnumbers those of other foreign countries. A study prepared by Prof. Chŏng Byŏng-Hee indicates that during the years 1950-1969 40 works by 28 American playwrights were performed followed by 35 by 17 British dramatists including the perennial Shakespeare and then came 22 by 14 Frenchmen and 17 by 15 Germans (Chŏng, "Performances of Foreign Plays in Korea: a Statistical Analysis," 1971). Of the individual playwrights, O'Neill stands out first with 25 performances of his 11 plays. According to another study, the one cited above, by Miss Kim Sung-A, there were 368 student performances during the period 1945-1969, of which 258, that is, roughly 70%, were of foreign stock, and one third of these foreign plays were of American origin. According to her list, by far the most frequently performed one-acter is *Ile* by O'Neill, and among the list of favorite plays are *Our Town, The Glass Menagerie, A View From the Bridge* and *Bus Stop*. Again, the present writer's investigation shows that during the years 1945-1970, 50 American plays by 25 authors altogether were performed by what in general were regarded as professional companies. Among these one finds such important figures as Maxwell Anderson, Sidney Kingsley, Lillian Hellman, George Kaufman, William Saroyan, Edward Albee and Murray Schisgal, not to mention O'Neill, Williams and Miller.

First, an analysis by the period will be helpful. As was already explained, the first true decade of American drama in

Korea started with the outbreak of the Korean War. But it was not until 1954 that the first flow of new American drama was introduced to the war-ridden people. In this year the first Korean performance of Miller's *Death of a Salesman* was made by a semi-professional troupe called 'Theatre-libre' (à la French, but more interested in American drama); 1955 also saw the first presentation of Williams' masterpiece *Streetcar Named Desire* by the Sinhyŏp, a company most representative of Korean theatre throughout the 1950s. Then followed a presentation of O'Neill's *Desire Under the Elms* by the same troupe. Unlike 1937 or 1949, for the first time a regularly scheduled season of major American works was intended, and this not without some success. With the rising reputation of this trio of leading American playwrights in Korea, a substantial portion of the Korean audience began to be intimate with American drama.

However, some critical remarks should be added here, particularly in the case of O'Neill. Since he arrived in the Korean theatre rather belatedly with a prolificacy hardly achieved by anybody at one time, the selection of plays to be performed was inevitably one-sided, whether this was caused by literary consideration, theatrical judgment or personal taste. Anyhow, the O'Neill plays chosen for the Korean theatre were unusually one-sided in their content and style. They were largely realistic in tone, appealing to the naive sense of what the audience assumed to be tragic in life, as was remarked earlier in this paper. Such a tendency of play selection honestly reflected the degree of awareness to which the theatre people in Korea had arrived at in those days, as to what the theatre is and should be in the modern world. They simply rejected any attempt at non-realistic approaches to the theatre. They failed to understand that art is more than life, that theatre is not the merely banal imitation of what we observe in life.

Moreover, the attachment to the realistic and 'tragic' in the theatre does not necessarily mean that they were successful in the staging of realistic pieces. On the contrary, partly because of the limitation in the actor's ability and partly because of the director's lack of insight, most of the serious American plays resulted in more or less a failure on the stage. Meanwhile, such plays as *Our Town, Matchmaker*, or even *The Glass Menagerie*, that is, plays which could dispense with an excessive overflow of emotional intensity were readily accepted. The only exception, to the present writer's knowledge, was *Long Day's Journey into Night* staged at the Seoul Drama Center in 1962. It was superbly done, and one could notice that the style of acting was essentially the continuation of the Sinhyŏp tradition.

The close relationship which the Sinhyŏp company maintained with modern American plays in the late 1950s was a remarkable one. Since the histrionic sensibility of the troupe was more akin to the eclectic style of a modern theatre based on psychological realism, it is most natural that they have formed an affection for the regular Broadway plays. These seemed more familiar to them than those European plays which were either stringent in form or delicate in dramatic nuance. Anyhow, it is hardly deniable that the Sinhyŏp contributed a great deal to American drama taking roots in Korean soil in the 1950s.

In the next decade, several important changes took place on the Korean stage. The first was the replacement of the older generation by the new. The first wave of the renewal process started around 1960. The newly emerged coteries were in general hostile to the Sinhyŏp tradition, though of course this did not necessarily mean an aversion to American drama. What they really wanted was to revive a spirit they found lacking on the stage — a spirit which would reflect the new waves of the contemporary theatre. Above all, they wanted freedom from the yoke of realistic drama and the right to experiment. They also looked forward to the birth of new Korean plays by the younger generation. Under such circumstances, it was most natural that the general repertory of plays performed were much different from those of former days. To cite an example, it was in 1960 that the first performances of Osborne's *Look Back in Anger* and the Absurdist play *The Lesson* by Ionesco were given in Seoul by two of the young troupes.

However, in so far as American drama is concerned, no new trend could be found to meet the changes witnessed in the 1960s. Rather, it may safely be stated that American drama itself was lost in the early 1960s so that hardly anybody would care about the emergence of a play equal in calibre to, say, *Streetcar* or *a Salesman* as it was esteemed in the late 1940s. It seems to me that such excellent American plays of the sixties as Albee's *Zoo Story* or *Who's Afraid of Virginia Wolf?* had lost the universal appeal which his predecessors once enjoyed in the fifties. As the drama of any period is forced to reflect the moral confusion and social unrest of a society engulfed in maelstrom, it becomes more and more restricted in scope and appeal. Though these two plays were enacted respectively in 1965 and 1967, the initial enthusiasm for American drama was lost. Still well publicized is American drama in Korea, compared with other European plays; 'Off Broadway' or even 'Off Off-Broadway' is a familiar term among theatre people in Seoul. There are, however, very few, if any, who want to introduce plays presented there or even attach any special importance to the plays themselves, except for the attempt itself. In 1971, there were two current American plays performed in a Korean theatre: Murray Schisgal's *Luv* and Neil Simon's *Odd Couple*. Both were the well-publicized Broadway successes and both were fairly well received by Korean audiences mostly young; both were light comedies bantering on contemporary American life, especially on urban life in Metropolitan New York. Such was the plight of American plays in Korea at the beginning of the seventies.

The Cinema in Korea:
A Robust Invalid

JAMES WADE

History and Background

A reviewer at the 1968 Cork (Ireland) Film Festival, approaching a South Korean[1] motion picture entry with obvious trepidation, seemed rather relieved to be able to report that "it could be classified as a pleasant surprise inasmuch as it reaches a technical standard comparable to a Japanese B production, and that's a compliment. Also, it proved never dull, another compliment."[2]

Whether or not the Koreans, with their long-standing dislike and jealousy of the Japanese, would consider this verdict flattering, it is probably a fair general evaluation of the current state of Korean cinema, and reflects — no doubt unintentionally — the close connection between the film histories of the two neighboring countries.

In all probability, the first showing of a motion picture in Korea occurred in 1904, during the period when Japan was maneuvering to establish a protectorate over the weak, backward "Hermit Kingdom."[3] Thus it is not surprising that this film is said to have been a primitive newsreel documenting the victory of the Japanese navy over the Russian fleet in the Sea of Japan, just off the Korean coast, during the brief Russo-Japanese War of that year. The sequence was in all likelihood shown privately to high-ranking Korean officials in an effort to convince them of Japan's invincibility, and therefore of the inevitability of the protectorate treaty.

About the same time (some say a year earlier), the first movie designed for the general public was introduced: a brief advertisement intended to promote an electric street car line just completed in Seoul by an American firm. This innovation had earned the disapproval of conservative Koreans, and the film sequence was evidently intended to help popularize the novel means of transport.

Imported Western-made films began to be shown in theater engagements during the following decades. Early hits with Korean audiences are remembered as "King of Kings," "Broken Blossoms," "Way Down East," Fritz Lang's Siegfried films, and Douglas Fairbanks as Robin Hood.

It is generally agreed that the first feature motion picture made in Korea was "Ch'un Hyang" ("Spring Fragrance") (1921)[4], an old legend of true love, long-suffering virtue, political corruption, and the ultimate triumph of Confucian principles. (This story, the most popular folk tale of the Korean people, has appeared in virtually every conceivable artistic form,[5] and has been filmed a total of seven times; its importance is such that we will return to a detailed consideration of it later, in an examination of the themes in Korean cinema.)

An important and unique innovation of this era was the employment in movie houses of a live story-teller called *pyŏnsa*, who explained the plot to the audience as the picture unreeled, and supplied dialogue for all the parts. The origins of this practice may perhaps be traced to the strolling player who from time immemorial had chanted long traditional ballad cycles called *p'ansori*, the principal theatrical diversion of the common people.

The *pyŏnsa* not only obviated the need for expensive subtitling, and translation of subtitles of foreign films; he was also able to inject into local films an element of political satire and protest against Japanese domination, which became outright oppression after the annexation in 1910. Thus the

1928 film "Arirang" (titled after a Korean folk song that, similarly, had no political overtones, but which nevertheless became a resistance symbol), made by the first great Korean actor-director, Na Un-gyu,[6] is considered patriotic and anti-Japanese, although this must certainly have resided more in the *pyŏnsa*'s explanations than in the film's visual elements, which the Japanese could censor, though they could scarcely control what the *pyŏnsa* might say in Korean, a language few Japanese ever learned to speak well.[7]

With the advent of sound films in 1928, the *pyŏnsa* of course began to disappear,[8] and Japanese movies — especially the early *samurai* epics — started to take over the Korean market, in part due to the Japanese government's policy to propagandize Korea with its new belligerence, which soon led to the 1937 "Manchuria Incident" and the subsequent invasion of China by way of Korea.

Nevertheless, Korean producers did make a few sound films before the war, the first being the inevitable "Ch'un Hyang" in 1935. From 1938 until the end of the Pacific War in 1945, cinema activities were exclusively in the hands of the Japanese, and directed entirely toward crude propaganda ends.

With liberation came political chaos and the tragedy of national division, the north being occupied by Soviet forces which set up a Communist dictatorship, and the south by the American army, which — lacking any practical policy directives from Washington — was never sure exactly what it was supposed to do, surrounded as it was by contentious local political factions that mushroomed after long suppression.

Despite the political and economic disruption, lasting until the establishment of the Republic of Korea government late in 1948, about 20 feature films (mostly silent, in 16 mm., though including a few 35 mm. entries) appeared in the five-year period before the Korean War. Almost all of these are recalled as being extremely inept, due to lack of equipment, experience, and financing. Only one, titled "Chayu Manse!" ("Hurrah for Freedom!") (1946), made a strong impression and started a cycle of nationalistic anti-Japanese films which — understandably in the circumstances — broke all box-office records, but which will be ignored here as being of negligible importance to the overall view of Korean cinema.

The Korean War (1950-1953) shattered the fledgling industry. Even the obsolete equipment and facilities previously available were lost or destroyed as large parts of the peninsula were fought over not once but in some cases three or four times. The movie industry was reborn only after the war, when the U.S. foreign aid program and several private foundations, realizing the importance of films as an educational and socially cohesive factor, brought in new equipment and set up a modern studio complete with sound stage.

These facilities were under ROK government control, but available on rental to qualified private producers. For its part, the government began producing newsreels for local consumption and documentary shorts for overseas publicity. Many fine cultural films have been made, an outstanding example of which is the film on Korean Buddhism called "Nirvana," produced by Yang Jong-hae, which won the prize as top documentary in the 1965 Asian Film Festival.

Soon after the government studio opened, a private movie center was also set up in Anyang, just south of Seoul. (It should be remarked here, perhaps, that by 1968 directors were again complaining of the obsolescence of equipment, especially the cameras, probably caused by overuse, carelessness, poor maintenance, and lack of spare parts and skilled repairmen.)

As a final catalyst precipitating the revival of the postwar Korean film industry, the government, also in 1955, removed the heavy entertainment tax from movietickets, for the first time making it possible for a successful film to be reasonably profitable to its makers.

The first smash hit in the Renaissance of Korean cinema was, predictably enough, "Ch'un Hyang" (1955), directed by Yi Kyu-hwan, which was seen 90,000 people during its

21-day first-run showing in Seoul. Composed in simple, graceful shots, with sharply contrasted black and white photography, well acted, artfully paced and cut, this version (in the opinion of the present writer) is the best of all post-war filmings of the celebrated story, and the first surviving Korean screen classic. Others may prefer the later color adaptations, but these seem to get slower and more elephantine all the time. Brevity, dictated by scarcity of film stock, may have helped make the 1955 version memorable!

The next year came a very different and even more popular hit, "Chayu Puin" ("Free Wife"), the story of a college professor's wife who flouts convention by having an extra-marital love affair. That this Korean equivalent of "A Doll's House" had such an immense success indicates that the rigid Confucian moral order was in process of change; but no systematic research has so far been undertaken to determine accurately the role of films in initiating or crystallizing such changes. It may be noted, however, that a group of college professors protested the showing of this film, on the grounds of general danger to public morals and specific defamation of their profession. This pattern of attempted suppression was to appear persistently at a later date.

In 1958, the first locally-processed feature film in color was completed. It is probably superfluous to mention that it was "Ch'un Hyang" again.[9] The initial full-length animated color cartoon, "Hong Kil-dong," a folk tale Disneyfied for children, came in 1967.

At the time of the revival of Korean sound films in 1955, nearly all movies used music tracks taken from pirated imported phonograph records, since Korea is not a member of the international copyright convention. Korea soon began to dispense with this practice, however, unlike other non-copyright areas such as Taiwan.[10] By the 1960's, most features boasted original sound tracks by leading composers such as Kim Dong-jin and Chŏng Yun-ju. The generally excellent scores are still handicapped by the use of undermanned, under-rehearsed pickup orchestras and slipshod recording techniques.

In the field of foreign film imports, the government has established an import quota to protect domestic producers. Through a rather complicated system, the minimum quota for imports is allocated among Korean producers on the basis of their own yearly numerical production levels, to which may be added various bonuses for producers whose products have been shown abroad, entered competitions, or won festival prizes. In the early 1960s, imported films approximately equalled domestic production; but foreign film imports have steadily declined since then (see Tables I and II).

Judging by recent imported hits, Korean audiences favor French and Italian love stories (though these are heavily cut in nude and erotic scenes), lurid documentaries of the "Mondo" series type, the Italian-made "macaroni" cowboy movies, and U.S. musical, crime, and Western dramas, approximately in that order. "Cleopatra" had a successful run, and the Disney True Life Adventures keep coming back over and over, with good audience response.

Due to the cautious government attitude in regard to recently (1966) re-established diplomatic relations with Japan, no commercial features from the neighboring country have been shown in Korea since 1945. The exceptions to this comprise entries, shown before invited audiences only, to the Asian Film Festivals held in Seoul in 1962 and 1966. To these, it is generally agreed, Japan sends "second-string" entries, both to avoid taking the lion's share of the prizes due to her technically more sophisticated productions, and also to save her best films for more prestigious festivals.[11]

Themes and Impact

The Korean film, apparently from its earliest examples over 40 years ago, has reflected the special qualities of the Korean people, sometimes known as "the Irish of the Orient," and the characteristics of their ancient theater arts: earthiness, irony, volatility, violence, nostalgia, and sentiment. Not that other peoples have failed to express their nature accurately in film and drama; but the modern Korean actor or director — deeply instinctive, extrovert, and unburdened by traditions of stylization or restraint — throws himself into film making with an uninhibited physical and temperamental involvement that evokes instant empathy in any audience.

The risk, in other words, is not that a Korean film will be dull or static, but that it may be flamboyantly melodramatic — to the point of caricature, so far as a Western audience is concerned. The best directors have avoided such excesses, and even approached New Wave boredom, whether deliberately or not; but the tendency remains marked in most films.

Every Korean movie, for instance, is equipped with at least one lengthy and harrowing scene of the heroine weeping. (Sometimes men will be drawn into such a scene in subordinate roles like that of the *premier danseur*; but, as in the case of ballet, it is essentially a virtuoso female performance.)

Sophisticated or westernized Koreans (the terms tend to be synonymous, at least when used by foreigners) deplore these crying jags, but the producers insist they must use such devices to guarantee popular success — and not only in rural areas.

There are also signs of a rather morbid dwelling upon wounds, torture, bloodshed and mortal illness in many movies.

Both these tendencies, of course, can be seen — and in more extreme form occasionally — in both Japanese and overseas Chinese films; and may have had their cinematic origin in these, so far as Korea is concerned. Also, parallel or overlapping common factors in the legends and traditions of all three countries suggest much earlier mutual influences, which have been documented exhaustively by scholars.

To glimpse the special Korean twist to these and other

themes, let us examine the perennial favorite "Ch'un Hyang," an 18th century story filmed seven times already, and still going strong.

The son of a provincial magistrate, Yi Do-ryŏng, meets Sŏng Ch'un-hyang, lovely young daughter of a former *kisaeng* (geisha) and thus socially unacceptable as the wife for a scholar-aristocrat. Nevertheless, they fall in love and marry secretly (upward social mobility is an important theme[12]). But Do-ryŏng's father is transferred to the capital, and Do-ryŏng must go too, in order to take the annual Confucian academy examinations that lead to political preferment.

The new magistrate, Pyŏn Sat-do, is a villain who squeezes the poor farmers and commandeers the fairest girls of the district to glut his sensuality. Hearing of the beauty of Ch'un-hyang, he sends for her, but she refuses to become his mistress, saying that she is already married. Pyŏn has her beaten and thrown into prison, threatening to execute her as part of the entertainment at his impending birthday banquet unless she accedes to his demands (political oppression and injustice are recurring themes in both Korean literature and cinema).

Do-ryŏng returns in rags as a beggar, stating that he has failed his examinations and been disowned by his father. He visits Ch'un-hyang in jail, and she has her obligatory weeping scene as the doomed wife faithful to death (marital fidelity is a much-valued traditional virtue in Korea — but only for wives).

However, Do-ryŏng has lied: having passed his examination with highest marks, he is now a secret emissary of the king, travelling in disguise to seek out and redress injustices. Thus at Pyŏn's birthday party Do-ryŏng interrupts and denounces the magistrate as an enemy of the people in an elegant, allusive Chinese poem that proves he is no illiterate beggar. Royal troops hidden nearby break in and the villain is led away to punishment, while Ch'un-hyang, rescued on the very brink of execution, is reunited with her husband for a future of bliss. (The theme of reform within the established system is an obvious corollary of Confucian thinking.)

That the hero let his wife believe until the last moment that she was about to be executed seems wantonly cruel, since he could have told her the truth, or at least held out some hope to her, during their clandestine meeting in the prison the night before. This suggests, when viewed with other similar cliff-hangers, that one major theme of Korean cinema is, "Women must suffer — that's what they're for." (Indeed, in one old version of the story, the heroine dies immediately after her rescue, of tortures received in prison.)

Traces of this theme in more up-to-date garb may be found in the fine comedy drama "Sarang Bang Sonnim Kwa Ŏmŏni" ("Mother and the Roomer"), directed by Shin Sang-ok, which won a top prize in the 1962 Asian Film Festival. The story takes place in the early modern period, and is seen largely through the uncomprehending eyes of a child.

A young widow rents her spare room to a handsome bachelor in order to make extra money. They fall in love, but the old-fashioned mores of the community frown on remarriage of a widow. They decide to part, rather than risk social ostracism and persecution of the woman's young daughter. This plot permits plenty of latitude for grief as well as comedy, as the little girl fails to understand the situation. It also provides a virtuoso part for the Cute Kid stereotype, of which Koreans are quite fond.

Suffering is again the theme in "Chi-ok Mun" ("Gate of Hell"; not to be confused with the Japanese film of the same title), directed by Yi Yong-min in 1962. A tyrant king during one of the ancient dynasties practices unheard-of cruelties, such as the graphic drowning of an enemy and his young son in an immense palace cesspool (Korean cruelty as well as humor tends toward the excremental). Finally the king and his evil cohorts die and go to the Buddhist hell, where they are visited by a monk who left the court and entered a monastery after being sickened by the abuses of the tyrant. The monk is traversing hell to bring absolution and salvation to the spirit of his dead mother, who had been one of the wicked courtiers.

The most effective scenes are those showing the tortures of the damned, done with excellent special effects, in color. Thus the film is an equivalent of the average Hollywood "Biblical spectacular," where a casual cloak of piety covers the real purpose: depiction of violence and depravity.

Following up the excremental humor theme for a moment, there is one memorable sequence in the first Korean science-fiction film, "Wang-magui" or "King-Size Monster" (1967). When the giant ape from outer space begins to tear down the scale model of Seoul in the accepted international ritual, a street urchin leaps from a collapsing building and lands atop the monster's head. He crawls into one ear, travels through the Eustachian tube (apparently) into the nasal passages, and peers roguishly out one immense nostril as the ape continues to destroy the city. Suddenly the monster halts, roars, and begins to slap madly at his head: the scene shifts to a fleeting shot of the boy urinating against the wall of its nasal passage![13]

Korean films, like those of other nations, tend to go in cycles. The earliest period, 1921-1938, seems to have comprised "modern problem" stories and a few old legends, with anti-Japanese elements suggested in the former as much as possible. After the immediate postwar orgy of anti-Japanism, the industry groped a long time before a new trend appeared: juvenile rebellion and glamorized gangsterism, in a cycle starting in the late 1950's. Most native observers agree that these films had a demonstrable — and unhealthy — effect on the speech, dress, and thinking patterns of Korean youth, producing a tough guy or would-be delinquent image as the social ideal. (The James Dean and motorcycle gang movies from the U.S. about this time may have had appreciable influence too.)

The number of actual war films has been surprisingly small, due to a combination of reasons. Staging modern battle scenes is prohibitively expensive, and depicting Communist characters is politically touchy, as several film-makers have learned to their regret. Even the Vietnam War, in which

Koreans are genuinely proud of their participation, has inspired few films.

The most successful military film was Shin Productions' "Ppalgan Mafula" ("Red Scarf") (1964), about the jet fighters of the ROK Air Force. The government assisted this production by providing the expensive aerial camera work and various stock footage.

Historical epics such as "Yŏnsan Kun" ("Prince Yŏnsan") (1961), directed by Shin Sang-ok, who might with some justice be called the De Mille of Korea, had a vogue in the early 1960's, followed by rather "arty" adaptations of modern literary pieces, such as "Manch'u" ("Late Autumn") (1967). These stressed melancholy moods, nostalgia, and doomed love, with misty atmospheric scenic effects and restrained, naturalistic acting.

Starting in 1966 there was even a brief fad for quasi-travelogues, led off by the Cinemascope and color feature "Paltogangsan" ("Sights of the Eight Provinces"; dubbed in English as "Six Daughters"). This film has an interesting origin: the government wished to produce an upbeat documentary stressing economic and social gains made under its aegis, as part of the buildup to the 1967 national elections. Pae Sŏk-in, a director of official documentaries, was assigned to the task, and top stars recruited. The finest facilities and equipment were made available, together with an unusually generous budget.

Realizing that the propaganda would have to be adroitly sugar-coated to be successful, Pae wrote a clever script in which a comic old couple sets out on a tour around Korea to visit six married daughters. Each episode includes an entertaining human vignette, a glimpse of regional development, and a scenic-musical travelogue, well integrated into the plot. Korea's most popular stars participated, headed by Kim Hi-kap, who has been playing foxy-grandpa roles so long that it is difficult to realize he is only in his mid-40's.

This film is an obvious example of the social-mobility

theme: Pae even cannily included one sequence of a family living in poverty and privation, all the while saving to invest in a fishing boat that would eventually boost them from rags to relative riches.

The picture was a smash box-office success, and the incumbent party won re-election, whatever the connection between the two facts may have been. But every Korean movie fad seems to burn itself out at meteoric speed, as director Pae found when he quit his government job to make further independent feature-documentaries that were only moderately successful.

The most tenacious type of Korean film, always popular when well done, is the family comedy-drama, sometimes based on well-known radio soap operas or newspaper serial stories. This genre is popular with foreign viewers, too, since the films usually have variety and pace, which many Korean movies lack.

The typical plot will involve the vicissitudes of a big family of three generations living in the same house (the sly, silly, bibulous, witty old grand-father is always Kim Hi-kap): parental problems, job troubles, in-law troubles (including the marrying off of a son or brother of the head of the house), and especially the generation gap, stressing all the imaginable scrapes newly-emancipated Korean youth might possibly get into.

The actors are lively and attractive, the tempo frenetic, the pantomime diverting, and nothing is taken too seriously, unless it is the Weeping Scene. The family is always of the upper-middle or lower-upper income group, underlining audience aspirations for self-improvement (somebody is always getting ready to go to the States), as well as general disapproval of the very rich, who appear in these films as loud-mouthed, vulgar bosses or *nouveau riche* snobs.

Twin Burdens: Financing and Censorship

Korean movies today are dominated by a rigidly stratified star system. The top dozen or so players, incredible as it may seem, sometimes act in as many as 20 to 30 different films shooting simultaneously. The competition for their services is so keen that they can command salaries of as much as $2,000 per picture, making them among the highest-paid of all Koreans, as revealed by income tax statistics.[14]

The reasons for this fantastic situation, and the cause of many long-standing deficiencies in Korean cinema, lie in the method of financing films, one of two major drawbacks the industry has yet to conquer.

Bank loans, source of most business and industrial funds in Korea, are not in general available for film financing, which is considered a risky and precarious investment. Money to make movies usually comes from the theater owners themselves, the only group with a vested interest in seeing to it that films are made at all.

The theater owners naturally have strong ideas about what succeeds at the box office, with perhaps more justification in experience than the famous "New York bankers" who tend to get all the blame for Hollywood's alleged mediocrity. The independent producer must sell the idea for a new film to a major theater owner in order to secure a loan, and the latter will be interested only if the services of big-name stars can be assured; and will also feel free to insist on changes in the scenario and screen play.

If the completed picture has a two-week first run, with an audience of from 50,000 to 60,000, it is considered a success. Profits are divided between producer and exhibitor a 65-35 percent or 70-30 percent basis. After paying back the loan, the producer is free to contract for second-run and provincial showings. If the first run was not successful, his profits from these later engagements must go to pay off the debt, and he often winds up in the red. (See Table III)

TABLE I
Number of Korean Feature Films Produced 1955-1968

1955- 16	1956- 36	1957- 47
1958- 92	1059-110	1960- 91
1961- 85	1962-114	1963-144
1964-148	1965-189	1966-124
1967-171	1968-212	

Sources: 1955-1959: Korea, Its Lands, People and Culture of All Ages (Hakwon-sa, Ltd., 1960); 1960-1966: Motion Picture Producers Association of Korea; 1967-1968: Ministry of Culture and Information.

TABLE II
Source and Number of Foreign Feature Films Imported by Korea 1960-1968

Year	U.S.	British	French	Italian	W. German	Other	Total
1960	93	6	22	10	1	3	135
1961	61	2	10	12	5	4	84
1962	69	3	5	5	3	1	86
1963	61	2	4	8	2	5	82
1964	36	4	8	10	—	3	61
1965	42	—	3	1	—	7	53
1966	40	2	5	10	1	4	62
1967	20	2	1	12	—	4	39
1968	40	1	3	4	—	6	54

Sources: 1960-1966: Motion Picture Producers Association of Korea: 1967-1968: Ministry of Culture and Information.

TABLE III
Number of Theaters and Attendance 1962-1966

Year	Number of Theaters	Total Attendance
1961	302	58,608,075
1962	344	79,046,162

1963	386	95,059,311
1964	477	104,579,315
1965	529	121,697,527
1966	534	156,336,340

Source: Korea Cinema 1967, published by Motion Picture Producers Assn. of Korea

Under these circumstances, as one movieman put it, the producer is a salesman first, impresario second, and an artist last, if at all. Only a few quality productions are undertaken each year, mostly in overseas competitions. The producers and even the public tire of the same faces of established actors, but the conservatism of the financiers inhibits giving new talent a break.[15]

An average production (1968) costs between 10,000,000 and 20,000,000 wŏn ($37,000 to $74,000 by 1968 exchange rates). Only 5 to 10 percent of this is paid as salary to director and technicians. Most of the rest goes for the actors, film stock, lab work, and editing, leaving a bare minimum for sets, costumes, and other niceties.

In such a situation, it is not surprising that every attempt must be made to conserve expensive imported film stock. Ratio of footage shot to that used is 2 to 1 on the average, never more than 6 to 1. In some cases, only 15,000 feet are shot to produce a 9,000-foot final print.

These figures refer to black and white shooting. In recent years, the popularity of color movies has elicited pressures for more of these, sharply increasing the already overburdened producers.

If the caution of theater owners constitutes a *de facto* censorship over Korean motion pictures, the outright censorship of the government, as exercised ostensibly by the Ministry of Culture and Information, is at least equally discouraging to serious film makers. All scenarios must be submitted for approval before filming, and finished prints are reviewed and arbitrarily cut without recourse.[16]

The government is empowered to control films in two broad areas: public morals and order, and politics specifically. In terms of practice, this latter category can be stretched to suppress any form of social criticism, satire, or realism. Thus a film about how inmates of an orphanage formed a successful football team and became famous suffered cuts in early scenes showing the poor living conditions of the orphans, leading the producer to ask, "Should I depict all orphans in Korea as living in a luxurious manner?"[17]

The niggling extends even to single words of titles, taken out of context: "The Black Cloud" was rejected because "the title was likely to damage the bright side of people's sentiments."[18]

In 1965, veteran director Yu Hyŏn-mok filmed Richard E. Kim's best selling English novel *The Martyred.*[19] This book embodies an implication of moral ambiguity, of greyness rather than sharp blacks and whites, in the story of a Christian minister suspected of having betrayed his colleagues to the Communists during the Korean War. The film's scenario and final print were approved by the censors, presumably because the suppression of movie based on a work by an internationally known author would have created a world-wide stir.

But four days after the film opened, a group of conservative Presbyterian clergymen — with or without encouragement from higher up — sued in court to have one-third of the film cut, on the basis of defamation of the clergy and encouragement to the Communists. Liberal sentiment in Korea rallied behind Yu, including the more enlightened elements among Presbyterians. Fear of adverse publicity abroad is also assumed to have played a part in saving the film from castration.

However, the authorities has not yet finished with Yu. The following year he directed an experimental film, "Ch'unmong" ("Spring Dream"), consisting largely of fantastic dreams done in an expressionist and surrealist manner reminiscent of "The Cabinet of Dr. Caligari" or "Spellbound" (the first such psychological fantasy in Korean cinema). The censors in examining this found fault with a simulated nude scene and some allegedly sadistic sequences. Not only was 400 feet of film, affecting 15 scenes, clipped from the print, but Yu was indicted on charges of making an obscene movie, despite the fact that the offending footage was never exhibited. (Other directors have tried their luck earlier with similar scene, always scissored, but without undergoing prosecution.)

The public prosecutor in Yu's trial was the same conservative Presbyterian attorney who had earlier led the campaign against "The Martyred."

During the trial, Yu contended that, as to the obscenity charge, certain foreign films shown in Korea had contained such scenes. The government replied that the imported movies were works of art, while Yu's was not. (The foreign films under discussion were "The Carpetbaggers" and an Italian 'skin show,' "Adam and Eve.")[20]

Yu paid a fine of just over $100 on the obscenity charge.[21] His actual penalty was light, but he had received the intended message. He has not made any further "controversial" movies since.

In response to the government's continued claim of "clear and present danger" as justification for all types of censorship (sincerely believed by some knowledgable Koreans), the movie makers as a whole contend that self-censorship within the industry would suffice.

"We film people have common sense," one well-known director told this writer. "If there were no censorship, there would be little tendency toward extremes. We too went through the Korean War, and we know more than enough about Communist cruelties to be able to show Communism as it really is, without needless exaggeration or childish distortion.

"There should be a committee of about 20 independent civic leaders set up to police the industry. At present, there is a so-called advisory council to the government of films, but in actual fact the decisions are made entirely by three government officials, who have no set standards, no ex-

perience in films, and no competence in artistic matters."
Despite nearly half a century of extreme vicissitudes, and
the chronic continued crises in which it presently exists, the
cinema in Korea has proved to be a robust invalid indeed. As
an industry it has survived and expanded; and as an art form,
it has helped enlighten, encourage, and entertain its public,
holding a mirror — however flawed — to the face of a society
in rapid, pandemonic transition, and preserving a
kaleidoscopic record of social change and historical upheaval.

Its future, if one may hazard a guess, looks just as perilous,
exciting, and unpredictable as its hectic past and present.

NOTES

The above article is adapted from a chapter in the forthcoming book,
Asian Film and Popular Cultures, edited by Charles Leslie, to be published
later in 1969 by the University of Chicago Press. The gist of this article was
delivered as a lecture before the Royal Asiatic Society Korea Branch, on
Feb. 26, 1969.

1. For obvious reasons, this essay can deal only with cinema in the Republic
   of Korea (South Korea), omitting any consideration of the Communist
   northern zone *terra incognita* for any American, except unlucky, un-
   willing guests such as the crew of the U.S. intelligence ship *Pueblo*.
2. *Variety*, Oct. 23, 1968. The film was reviewed under the title "True
   Love," though the Korean title, "Memil Kkot P'il-muryŏp," translates
   "When the Buckwheat Blossoms."
3. This was accomplished in 1905, with full annexation coming in 1910
   and lasting until the end of World War II in 1945.
4. Some claim that "Wŏlha ŭi Maengse" ("Oath Under the Moon")
   came first, and assign "Ch'un Hyang" to 1922.
5. Including oral ballad cycle, drama, traditional opera, three Western-
   style grand operas (one by a Japanese composer), several comic parodies,
   and two Broadway-style musicals (one by an American Jesuit).
6. Na died prematurely of tuberculosis in 1937, and in true Hollywood
   fashion was recently honored with a biographical film on his life, also
   called "Arirang" (1966).
7. No prints of any pre-1945 Korean films survive, so any evaluation or
   description of them is entirely guesswork.

8. The usage may in a sense be said to survive in the present practice of professional voice actors dubbing sound tracks instead of the stars who appear on the screen.

9. Two more Cinemascope and color remakes of this durable classic had appeared by the mid-1960s, as well as a wild black and white spoof, in which the traditionally garbed characters rode in convertibles, drank Scotch, and danced to a juke box.

10. In the 1966 Asian Film Festival held in Seoul, the jury awarded the Best Music award to the "composer" credited with the score of the Taiwan entry "Orchid," oblivious of the fact that the music had been pieced together from recordings of Rachmaninoff, Wagner, Saint-Saens, etc.

11. But the exception in turn to this occurred in the 1962 festival, when Japan sent the brilliantly photographed "Ueo Muite Arukō" ("Keep Your Chin Up"), inventively directed by Toshio Masuda—an upbeat forerunner, in a sense, of "West Side Story" (Which in its film version had then yet to appear). This fine movie launched the meteoric Occidental career of Japanese singer Kyu Sakomoto, whose performance of the film's catchy theme song in Japanese later made a hit in U.S. record markets under the meaningless title "Sukiyaki." Festival audiences in Seoul heard it first! (The present writer has always wondered why the Japanese did not dub and export this exhilarating, if rather simplistically sentimental, film.)

12. CF *Korea: The Politics of the Vortex* by Gregory Henderson: Harvard University Press, 1968.

13. The picture was a commercial flop: apparently the Koreans are not as fond of the cinematic spectacle of their cities being destroyed as the Japanese—perhaps harboring a guilt complex—seem to be, judging by Godzilla and his many quaint successors.

14. The question of whether Korean movie stars have strong influence over their public is moot; but that international stars have strong influence on Korean stars is indicated by the fact that, at the height of the Elizabeth Taylor-Richard Burton affair, the Korean screen idols Kim Ji-mi and Ch'oe Mu-ryong offered their own version, which got them temporarily jailed for adultery in rather puritanical Korea. (See Time, Nov. 16, 1962. p. 31.)

15. Dominance of the established star system, and shakiness of financing, are suggested by the saying in Korean movie circles: "For location shooting, actors travel in their own cars, the director in a taxi, and the producer by bus."

16. See *New York Times,* Feb. 11, 1968, "Seoul Is Vigilant on Film Industry," p. 10.

17. *Korea Times,* June 9, 1968.
18. *Korea Times,* May 19, 1968.
19. Geo. Braziller, Inc, 1964.
20. *Korea Times,* Feb. 12, 1967.
21. *Korea Times,* Mar. 16, 1967.

Korea's Film World: History and Trends

JAMES WADE

Korean cinema, after many years in Limbo and nearly as many in the doldrums, has begun to receive a degree of recognition internationally in fairly recent times. One indication of this is the special screening in several cities of the United States of five Korean feature films and one made-for-TV hour-long musical drama under the auspices of the Asia Society of New York as part of the year-long centennial observance of Korean-American relations.

Coincidentally, this takes place in the sixtieth anniversary year of the first feature film produced in Korea.

The oldest of the five features was made in 1965; there are no extant "historical" Korean films, due to the chaotic times experienced in the latter days of the Japanese occupation (1910-1945) and the Korean War (1950-1953). Some stills and plot summaries survive, however, from the era before 1955, which is considered to mark the rebirth of Korea's film industry, and from this older material the Asia Society, in co-operation with the International Cultural Society of Korea, has put together an informative booklet entitled "Korean Cinema: Pictorial Survey," which includes an historical introduction and notes on some of the principal film artists of the past six decades.

It has sometimes been claimed that the first Korean cinematic drama was produced in 1919, but this was a so-called "kino-drama," or stage play with motion picture insertions, a bastard form which flourished for about four years, until true feature films began to appear.

The first movie films seen in Korea were newsreel documentaries of Japanese naval victories in the Russo-Japanese War of 1904, brought in by the Japanese to impress (or intimidate) Korean governmental leaders. About the same time, the initial public offering was introduced: a brief advertising film intended to promote an electrical street car line just completed in Seoul by an American firm.

The pioneer feature film, probably shot in 1921 but apparently released in 1922 was, appropriately enough, *Ch'unhyang-jŏn* ("Spring Fragrance," sometimes rendered with unconscious irony as "Spring Flagrance"), an old legend of true love, long-suffering virtue, and the ultimate triumph of Confucian principles. This story, the most popular quasi-folk tale of the Korean people, has been filmed about a dozen times so far, as well as appearing in oral ballad cycles (*p'ansori*), traditional opera, grand opera, operetta, and several comic parodies. (Composers supplying the music included a Japanese and an American Jesuit priest, besides Koreans.)

Ch'unhyang has been and remains so popular, one hazards, because the twin themes of upward social mobility and the possibility of punishing corrupt, tyrannical officials have appealed greatly to Koreans in modern times.

One often reads that early Korean films had definite patriotic and anti-Japanese overtones; and one wonders how this could be, in view of the parallel claims about the ruthless Japanese suppression of anything that ran counter to their annexation policy.

The resolution of this seeming contradiction lies in the institution of the *pyŏnsa*, or narrator, who obviated the need for subtitling of either domestic or imported movies. This person, who perhaps partook in some degree of the function of the *p'ansori* singer, or the performer of the *muga* (narrative) section of the shaman chant, "dubbed" all the parts live, and in all probability voiced the inarticulate sentiments of his audiences, injecting into local films that were pictorially innocuous elements of political satire and protest against Japanese exploitation.

Thus the 1928 film *Arirang* was named after a Korean vocal ballad the words of which have no political overtones, but following the film, the song became a resistance symbol like the Beethoven "V-for-Victory" theme in World War II, and is still considered patriotic.

This film served to introduce writer-director-actor Na Un-gyu, the first and still the most phenomenal "genius" of Korean film, in the Orson Welles category, who made 16 movies before his premature death in 1937. His output, none of which remains aside from some stills, was uneven; nevertheless, he is remembered as having been continually growing and experimenting up to the very end. (His death at 35 was due to tuberculosis.)

Na's career bridged the gap involving the introduction of sound, which occured in 1935, the first "talkie" being, predictably enough, *Ch'unhyang-jŏn*. However, from 1938, with the Pacific War casting its shadows ahead of it, all cinematic activity was placed in the hands of the Japanese overlords, and movies degenerated into chauvinistic propaganda. (With the advent of sound, the *pyŏnsa* of course was out of a job, and the injection of anti-Japanese material would have been well-nigh impossible.)

After Liberation in 1945, there was a flurry of activity in the Korean film industry, its first commercial success being a patriotic film of 1946 entitled, with disarming directness, *Chayu manse!* ("Hurrah for Freedom!"). This spawned a host of simplistic imitations, with no particular elements of quality recalled by those who were viewers at the time. However, the Korean War cut short any cinematic activity, and so thoroughly ruined and despoiled existing facilities that it was not until 1955 that the industry began to recover, assisted by two factors: the supply of new equipment under foreign aid programs, and the elimination of the entertainment tax on movie tickets.

In 1955, a new, visually beautiful and artistically restrained version of — yes, *Ch'unhyang* broke box office records by attracting an audience of 90,000 in a 21-day first-run showing in Seoul. The director was Yi Kyu-hwan, a veteran of silent days who, though he remained sporadically active until his death in 1982 at the age of 78, never again achieved a comparable success.

In 1956 a very different type of film captured public fancy, *Chayu puin* (Free Wife), the story of the neglected wife of a college professor who flouts convention by having an extra-marital love affair. (Groups of college professors, among other guardians of traditional morality, protested the showing of this Korean version of "A Doll's House" as a danger to the public and an insult to their profession.)

In 1958, the first locally-produced feature film in color appeared. It is probably superfluous to mention that it was *Ch'unhyang* again. The initial full-length animated color cartoon, *Hong Kil-dong*, the story of a kind of Korean Robin Hood, Disneyfied a folk tale for children in 1967.

The first Korean film shot in Cinemascope was released in 1961, giving lovely *Ch'unhyang* back to any members of the audience who had begun to miss her.

The ensuing two decades were largely a time of stagnation for Korean cinema, due to several converging factors. First, public interest lagged in the wake of the introduction of television, which discouraged both experiment and high-quality, high-budget conventional features. Second, government censorship, direct and indirect, prevented Korean directors from attempting anything in the least degree controversial or experimental. The only box office successes of this era tended to be primitive "kung fu" films, melodramatic domestic soap operas, youth comedies of horseplay and hormones, and tried-and-true historical-patriotic subjects.

Aware of the ailments of the movie industry, the government tried a number of remedies including the establishment of a National Film Promotion Corporation in the late 1970's in an attempt to distribute subsidies fairly to deserving film makers who might elevate the quality of the national product, without restriction by political circumstances.

Perhaps in part because of public boredom with low-quality TV, this pattern of stimulus began to bear fruit by the early 1980's. Most of the more highly esteemed Korean productions that have drawn favorable attention abroad (and, more important, succeeded at home) have come from that recent period, with a few notable exceptions. (It is also an important consideration that technical standards of the Korean cinema have improved steadily over the years.)

A telling comparison may be found in reading two reviews from *Variety*, the hard-headed, commercially-oriented American trade journal. The first, reviewing the film "True Love" (Korean title: *Memilkkot p'il muryŏp*, more properly translated as "When the Buckwheat Blossoms") at the 1968 Cork Film Festival, states, "It could be classified as a pleasant surprise inasmuch as it reaches a technical standard comparable to a Japanese B production, and that's a compliment. Also, it proved never dull, another compliment."

The second and more recent article, in the issue for December 30, 1981, deals with *P'imak* ("House of Death" or "The death Cottage" in the Asia Society titling), a considerable domestic success that year, and is considerably less condescending, calling it "a finely-wrought love story...in exquisite visual form" which "could find more fest (festival) outlets and some specialized outings (exhibitions) on its sheer beauty." The reviewer goes on to observe, however, that "there is a decidedly Japanese influence in framing, décors and even timing."..."Direction and playing," the reviewer avers, "plus playing, costumes and music are also assets."

P'imak is, in fact, one of the five films on the Asia Society exhibition list, and it might be of some interest to describe and analyze these features, as a sort of random cross section of Korean movies of the most recent era. They may not be in any statistical sense typical, but they are perhaps among the best examples of the most popular genres, with the exception of modern comedy.

Taking the films chronologically, the first to be made is *Kaetmaŭl* ("Seaside Village"), directed by Kim Su-yong in 1965. This is the only one of the group to be shot in black and white. (Although color had been available since 1958, its eschewal here may have had combined aesthetic and economic causes.)

This film typifies at the simplest level a very prevalent theme in Korean cinema and literature: the dilemma of a young widow in pre-modern or semi-modern times, as to whether to remarry, which would be an abomination, worthy of ostracism or even death, according to the strict Confucian canon. This situation is set forth amid the austere beauties of a coastal fishing village where the young wife of a drowned fisherman is being pursued by the town rake.

As their affair veers out of control, the formerly tradition-minded mother-in-law of the girl in effect urges her to leave town with her man, withholding any harsh judgement. But when the couple marry they face a difficult inland world as outcasts, and at last the husband is killed in a lumbering accident. The wife buries him and returns to her former in-laws in the fishing village, knowing she will never leave it again.

The moral, if any, seems to be that the old ways may be best; at least in the sense that newfangled ideas don't necessarily work out either.

Changma ("Rainy Season"), directed in 1979 by Yu Hyŏn-mok, one of the most consistently creative and original Korean cinema artists, is taken from a famous short story of the Korean War. During the Communist invasion in the summer of 1950, a refugee family from Seoul flees south to safety with in-laws of a farming village. The two grandmothers each have one son respectively in the Red and South Korean army. (This sounds overly schematic, but is done plausibly; and actually happened in reality many times.)

The tensions of war, and the choking heat of the rainy season, rendered in appropriately lush visual imagery, cause a falling out between the two families. When the Communist son is rumored dead, his mother consults a fortune teller who venally assured son still lives. The old woman, trusting the soothsayer, prepares a lavish banquet for the son she assumes will soon be home, but he fails to arrive, and she collapses from the nervous strain.

Suddenly a large, wounded snake appears, obviously the psychopomp of the dead man, and the other grandmother, forgetting the feud, offers the snake some of the food, almost as in a memorial rite, assuring it that its mother and family are well, and that it can go away in peace. (Veteran actress Hwang Chŏng-sun masterfully underplays this scene, never raising her voice, never losing the intensity.) The snake departs; the old women are reconciled.

The film is effectively seen, in part, from the viewpoint of one of the grandchildren, an eight-year-old boy, who enters into the action of the fairly complicated plot, much condensed here.

If this movie has any 'meaning' beyond its story, it is simply to emphasize the pervasive and continuing influence of Shamanism and its rites, consciously and unconsciously, in the lives of modern Koreans, a subject that has had some belated public recognition of late in the arts and entertainment media.

Shamanism is again the theme of *P'imak*, along with the young-widow theme examined earlier. The film was made in 1981 by Director Yi Tu-yong.

Again it is quasi-modern times. The son of the local rural aristocrat lies mysteriously ill; it is feared he will die young, like many of his male forebears, and a shaman sorceress is engaged to exorcise the evil that inhabits him. She sees in a vision and we see in flashback its origin: a young widow of the family, by stabbing her thigh to distract herself from carnal desire (a gruesome convention in many stories and films), develops an infection and is taken to the outlying "death cottage" where sick people go to prevent their spirits from haunting the family after death.

The girl's mother-in-law instructs the keeper of the Death Cottage to have sexual relations with the girl before she dies, so her ghost will not return out of frustration and harass the family. Reluctantly, he does so. But the girl recovers under his ministrations, their affair continues, and they have a child.

This outraging of Confucian virtue causes the family to have both of them murdered, and it is their spirits that curse the males of the line. Moreover, the sorceress brought in to cure the sick man is the daughter of the murdered couple! Horrendous events occur in rapid succession and there is a powerful, fiery exorcism at the end.

Again, the conflict of old and new values, and the stubborn persistence of Shamanism, underlie the story.

Manch'u ("Late Autumn") is a re-make of a famous earlier film, based on a well-known short story, directed by Kim Su-yong in 1981.

The plot is simple. A woman who murdered her brutal husband in a jealous rage is paroled from prison for a few days to perform the memorial rite at her mother's grave, accompanied by a woman guard. On the train she meets a charming roughneck who thaws her into humanity again after the frozen dehumanization of prison life.

They elude the guard and go to a hotel, where their love-making is extremely graphic by Korean standards, which until lately have been fixated at about the level of "The Outlaw."

The woman surrenders once more to the matron and goes back to prison, the lovers promising to meet exactly one year later at the time of the woman's release. But as has been hinted before, and as we see when the prison gates have closed behind her, the man too is a wanted criminal, and is arrested for a big robbery which will keep him incarcerated far longer than one year. The film ends as the woman waits for her lover in vain.

Several conclusions might be drawn: their love was ennobling to them but doomed because it was illicit, or because they were malefactors, or both. In any case, the soap opera ambience is overcome by extremely skillful performance and direction, and rural settings that are almost *too* pretty. (This was a criticism of those who had seen the first, "classic" version, and felt that this one sentimentalized it.)

The last and most recent film to be examined here is *Mandara*, directed by Yim Kwŏn-t'aek from a controversial novel, in 1981. This is perhaps the most mature and substantial Korean film made thus far, by a director who affirms his Koreanness unsparingly, even appearing "anti-Western" so far as cinematic influence goes. (Of foreign directors, he acknowledges only Kurosawa as master.)

The film consists of vignettes — some black comedy, some existentially philosophical — that relate the wanderings of two "unchurched", more or less renegade Buddhist monks. They plunge into the fleshpots, literally as well as figuratively, seeking to exhaust the excesses of sensualism in order to reach the divine that is imminent in everything, much as taught by certain esoteric sects of Sŏn (Zen) Buddhism.

In the end, one dies and the other cremates him in a winter setting or spectacular beauty that grows from the mood of the events — that is their *mandara* or *mudra* perhaps — rather than being superimposed decoratively. To ask for meanings here would be as crass as to parse the logic of a *koan*. Acting and direction share an intensity rare in any cinematic experience, and nearly unique in the fledgling film world of Korea.

Perhaps enough has been suggested in the foregoing to indicate that the Korean cinema has reached that well-known and sought-after "take-off stage" that we hear so much about in other fields. (Certainly this is true in terms of a relaxation of prudery.) Whether this means that its aesthetic achievement, its entertainment value and its commercial success will grow commensurately in the future is of course a moot question. But the Korean film industry has survived enough hard knocks in the past to endure a few more vicissitudes in the future, and seems to know where it is going. It will be interesting to follow it as it reels along through time to come.

Contributors in This volume

Han Man-yŏng   Professor of Korean Classical Music, Seoul National University

Sŏng Kyŏng-nin   Director, Classical Music Institute, Seoul

Eleanor King   Professor Emeritus of Dance, University of Arkansas, USA, Fulbright scholar

Christine Loken   Dance Ethnologist, Fulbright scholar Professor, Seoul Junior Teachers' College

Yi-Tu-hyŏn   Professor of Korean Folk Art, The Teachers' College of Seoul National University

Yu Min-yŏng   Professor of Korean Literature, Dankook University, Seoul

Yoh Suk-kee   Professor of English Language and Literature, Korea University, Seoul

James Wade   Mr. Wade, deceased, Journalist, Playwright, Composer, Poet, resided in Korea from 1960–1983